MW00324083

Broken Promise:

The Plight of
Our National Trails

Copyright ©2021 by Jim Kern

No part of this publication may be reproduced or transmitted in any form or by any means electronic or mechanical, including photocopying, recording, or by any information storage and retrieval system, without written permission of the author.

ISBN 978-0-5788-6720-5 (paperback)

Also by this author
The Wildlife Art and Adventures of Jim Kern Photographer
Trail Reflections, 50 Years of Hiking and Backpacking

Published by Kern House Publishing LLC
700 Island Landing Drive
St. Augustine, FL 32095
(904) 829-1515

kernhousepublishing.com

Printed in the U.S.A.

Book Layout: Caroline Blochlinger (cbAdvertising.com)

"We need to copy the great Appalachian Trail in all parts of America."

~President Lyndon B. Johnson, February 8, 1965

President Johnson signed the National Trails System Act on October 2, 1968

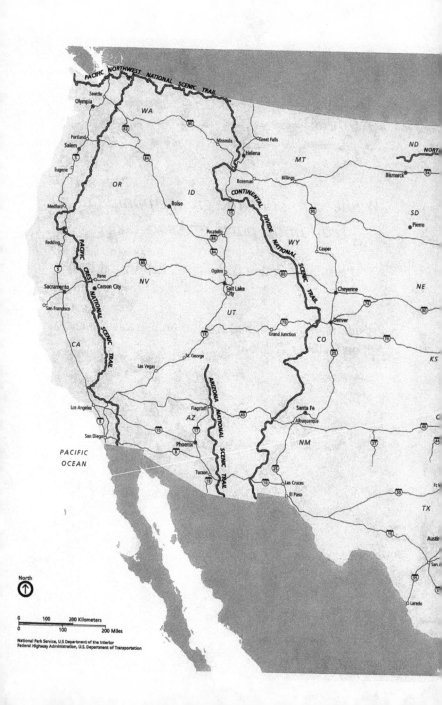

NATIONAL SCENIC TRAILS

Broken Promise:

The Plight of
Our National Trails

*An Appeal to the U.S. Congress
on Behalf of 47.9 Million* Hikers*

JIM KERN
PRESIDENT, HIKING TRAILS FOR AMERICA

CONTENTS

A National Trails System

There were two primary provisions in the National Trails System Act of 1968:

1. Acquire and preserve for posterity the right-of-way of the Appalachian Trail (A.T.).

2. Establish a category of iconic trails that would receive National Scenic Trail designation, a true system of trails. Congress had its eye on the Pacific Crest Trail (PCT), which was specifically named in the act as a second choice to receive this designation.

At first the implementation of the act was a bit of a struggle. Congress turned to the 14 states through which the A.T. passed and asked each of them to acquire its portion of the footpath. Maryland, Massachusetts, New Jersey, Pennsylvania and Virginia[1] were doing their part, but it is fair to say that the act was not accomplishing its stated purpose.

Congress wanted to know why, so a decade later, in 1978, it held oversight hearings on how it could be fixed. That's about the time I got involved. I received a phone call from Bill Kemsley, founder and owner of Backpacker magazine. He wondered if I would come to Washington to testify at these oversight hearings, as to why foot trails were important to America.

The turnout was poor. Bill and I were there. Paul Pritchard, Deputy Assistant Director of the U.S. Department of the Interior, was there, and so was Destry Jarvis, at that time representing the National Parks and Conservation Association. Surprisingly, the Appalachian Mountain Club made no appearance, nor did the Sierra Club, nor did the Audubon Society. In fact, most of the appropriate nonprofits were missing. (Note: It was the first time that Kemsley, Pritchard and I met. The hearings led soon after to the founding of the American Hiking Society by our threesome.)

The 1978 amendment took the task of acquisition away from the states and handed it to the National Park Service, with Dave Richey in charge of acquisition. At this point, things got rolling. Only two-thirds of the Appalachian Trail was on public land; about 700 miles had to be acquired in 2,550 parcels.[2] Each state had its own real estate challenges for buyer and seller. There was never a uniform contract. Every transaction had to be negotiated as a one of a kind. Dave Richey had tact and patience, which helped tremendously in the acquisition period. The process took about 30 years, and today the trail is now complete and secure, all 2,190 miles of it.

With the exception of the Arizona Trail, which lies predominantly within public land, the other nine iconic trails in this National Trails System are not complete. All have gaps. Significant gaps. That's because they do not have the critical section in their legislation that secured the Appalachian Trail. The A.T. had eminent domain. My friends in the hiking community are undeterred. They expect to complete their trails through "public and private partnerships." Negotiating rights-of-way— even with eminent domain—is a fraught exercise. How they will succeed, I do not know.

Some statistics will help the reader. In the chart that follows you will see each of the 10 trails identified, the number of miles in each and the miles of gaps. These gaps are usually spread out along the entire corridor. In the Florida Trail, for example, the 447 miles of gaps shown consist of about 2,850 separate parcels.[3] By the way, most of those 447 miles in Florida have to be walked on paved roads that are hot, boring and dangerous.

National Scenic Trail	Trail Length (Miles)	Gaps (Miles)	Gaps (%)
Arizona National Scenic Trail	807	None	None
Continental Divide National Scenic Trail	3,100	744	24%
Florida National Scenic Trail	1,584	447	28%
Ice Age National Scenic Trail	1,230	564	46%
Natchez Trace National Scenic Trail	65	None	N/A
New England National Scenic Trail	215	73	34%
North Country National Scenic Trail	4,702	1,988	42%
Pacific Crest National Scenic Trail	2,650	248	9.4%
Pacific Northwest National Scenic Trail	1,200	300	25%
Potomac Heritage National Scenic Trail	710	108	15%
Total (without the A.T.)	**16,263**	**4,472**	**27.5%**

Note: These numbers have fluctuated slightly over the years and are measured in different ways.

Further note: Trail mile lengths are important to two separate groups: thru-hikers and those who maintain trails. Thru-hikers on the Florida Trail will decide to go east around Lake Okeechobee or west around the lake. They must decide whether to go east around Orlando or west around the city. Their shortest hike from the southern terminus in Big Cypress National Preserve to Gulf Islands National Seashore east of Pensacola is 1,108 miles. The Florida Trail Association must maintain both loops and side trails as well, 1,584 miles. Elsewhere, we will use the mileage that is most appropriate for the context.

And so we have one complete trail, the oldest (the A.T.); one anomaly (the Arizona National Scenic Trail); and nine more that are incomplete, including a second anomaly, the Natchez Trace Trail. Our National Trails System is divided: one queen and 10 pretenders. Sadly, it will remain like this forever ... unless Congress acts.

Congratulations to the Pacific Crest Trail Association (PCTA) and The Trust for Public Land for closing on the $14 million purchase of land in the Trinity Divide, in 2019, which added 17 noncontiguous miles,[4] part of the 1/10 they still must acquire. The problem is that most trail clubs have had a good year if they can acquire five or 10 miles. In 2017 the PCTA, for example, acquired only 1.56 acres and it cost them $2.5 million.[5] They got some "viewshed" in the bargain, but the *sine qua non* is the treadway and its preservation.

This Trinity Divide sale just mentioned could have gone the other way. The purchase included a mountain lake with a cabin along its shoreline. The next time around, some truly wealthy person might be willing to pay double an appraisal for such a property, which would leave all the nonprofits in California on the outside, with their jaws agape. As it was, a broker involved in the transaction thought the PCTA paid a premium. With eminent domain available, the acquiring agency is required to pay "just compensation," but *not more than that!*

Again, looking at the chart, you will see that the gaps are staggering—over 25% of the total alignment acknowledged by Congress as the route for these 10 trails.

As a result of the favored position that the A.T. now occupies, many more people want to hike it than hike the others. (The Pacific Crest Trail, at the opposite end of the continent, is the exception. It can be hiked from end-to-end, but about 175 miles remain to be protected.) We should all agree that continuity is the single greatest attraction of the A.T. It can't be the trail itself, which hikers refer to as "the green tunnel." It can't be the grade of the trail, in places arduous and much steeper than our western grades designed to accommodate horses. It can't be the overlooks, which don't compare with spectacular views on the PCT and the Continental Divide Trail (CDT). Even our pancake-flat Florida Trail (FT) has grand vistas of open spaces for hikers crossing the Big Cypress Preserve, the Lake Kissimmee and Three Lakes Ranch sections and the St. Marks Refuge, to name only four.

How can the division just referred to ever be changed? How do we bring our 10 poor sister trails up to A.T. standards? Why are we calling these 10 trails National Scenic Trails at all? Completing every trail would bring bargain benefits, but the hiking community—at the rate it's going—won't get the job done. On top of all this, there is a mood throughout the hiking leadership that our National Scenic Trails can be completed with the legislation that is already in place. In the pages ahead, we will see that it's not possible. The lack of progress, after 42 years, should be clear to all of us.

2

Inequities Emerge

An important accomplishment of the 1978 act was the creation of a category of Historic Trails, something that should have been in the original act. Hiking trails and historic trails are well represented in America by the Partnership for the National Trails System.

Here is the list of 19 National Historic Trails supported by PNTS:

Ala Kahakai Trail	California Trail
Captain John Smith Chesapeake Trail	El Camino Real de Tierra Adentro Trail
El Camino Real de los Tejas Trail	Iditarod Trail
Juan Bautista de Anza Trail	Lewis and Clark Trail
Mormon Pioneer Trail	Nez Perce (Nee-Me-Poo) Trail
Old Spanish Trail	Oregon Trail
Overmountain Victory Trail	Pony Express Trail
Santa Fe Trail	Selma to Montgomery Trail
Star-Spangled Banner Trail	Trail of Tears Trail
Washington-Rochambeau Revolutionary Route	

Our Historic Trails may be "foot or horse paths, travel routes, roadways, or a combination," retracing routes that are a part of American history. Continuity and protection of a permanent route was never intended to be an essential aspect of Historic Trails, although there are voices today that speak up for continuity. What I find most useful are the large roadside panels that inform the public that the "Pony Express crossed here" or that South Pass City, WY, was our historic Grand Central Station for most of the trails westward.

Lastly, PNTS also supports National Recreation Trails. These are local and regional trails that may exist on both public and private land. Their key aspect is that their existence is conditional. They may be relocated or abandoned. Nevertheless, there are hundreds of such trails in America. They are an important part of our trail inventory.

The issue of continuity for our various foot trails is most serious for our National Scenic Trails because of their stature. No sooner was the A.T. completed, than hikers started talking about a hike from end-to-end. According to Larry Luxenberg in *Walking the Appalachian Trail,* MacKaye, the founder, "derided thru-hikes as 'stunts.' " Others agreed, but in 1948 Earl Shaffer did it... and made headlines. The Appalachian Trail Conference urged people to register before attempting a thru-hike. A thru-hike is not a stunt. It is a remarkable athletic achievement. It also dramatically illustrates the growing importance of hiking trails in America. But hikers want hikes without gaps. More on that later.

The following list dramatizes the importance of building a continuous trail. Preregistrations of thru-hikers on some National Scenic Trails are shown below. The first (A.T.) and the last (PCT) preregistrations swamp the numbers of the middle three, because even though these two trails are much longer than two of the other three, they are continuous.

National Scenic Trails Thru-Hiker Registration	Trail Length in Miles	2019 Registered (Completed)	2018 Registered (Completed)	2017 Registered (Completed)
Appalachian National Scenic Trail	2,190	7,881 (970[1])	6,532 (1,128)	6,717 (1,160)
Arizona National Scenic Trail	807	700[2] (100[3])	700 (103)	700 (114)
Continental Divide National Scenic Trail	3,100	100s (153)	100s (90)	100s (95)
Florida National Scenic Trail	1,584	30 +/- (30)	30 +/- (34)	30 +/- (34)
Pacific Crest National Scenic Trail	2,650	5,441 (919)	4,991 (1,177)	3,928 (537)

1. Numbers for 2019 are incomplete due to the coronavirus pandemic, per the Appalachian Trail Conservancy (ATC).

2. Permits are not required for a long-distance hike along the Arizona Trail. AZT Association estimates 700 thru-hikers per year: https://www.pbs.org/newshour/nation/hikers-fight-plan-for-building-border-wall-at-the-start-of-scenic-arizona-trail. However, since 1982, the Arizona Trail Association has documented more than 425 people who have completed all 807 miles of the trail. https://azdailysun.com/entertainment/arizona-trail-day-marks-50-years-of-national-trails-system/article_d566a6cb-159b-5824-af38-d3df92df590a.html

3. Only about 100 people thru-hike the Arizona Trail each year, with about half going northbound and the other half going southbound. https://www.greenbelly.co/pages/arizona-trail-map-planning-a-thru-hike

I attended the formative meeting of the PNTS shortly after the passage of the act. I was concerned then as to how hikers could fit under the same roof with mountain bikers and horse riders and who knew then how many others. Snowmobilers use trails, for example. The fact is that hikers have a severe affinity for quiet and for privacy that makes them uncomfortable with other trail users, particularly the noisy ones. A quote from the early days of the A.T., also from Luxenberg's book, supports that:

> "Remote for attachment,
> Narrow for chosen company,
> Winding for leisure,
> Lonely for contemplation,
> The Trail leads not merely
> North and south,
> But upward to the body, mind
> And soul of man."

Luxenberg adds that two out of three long-distance hikers are introverts. But hikers should be forgiven their elitist attitude. They scout, clear, blaze and annually maintain their resource. Then they open their trails to everyone.

Shortly after I founded Hiking Trails for America in 2013, I heard from several leaders of the hiking community that funding for land acquisition was the urgent need; we had more rights-of-way offered to us than we had money. I remember thinking at the time that such might not be the case.

Then an email arrived from Steve Elkinton of the National Park Service. I was a little late to the game, Steve advised. More land was available for us to buy than hikers had funds, and the Land and Water Conservation Fund had come through with $28 million in one year. It was a remarkable success for trails leadership. Kern, take it easy and go for a hike. The hikers, as you can see, know how to get these federal dollars if they try. Matters will take care of themselves; everything will work out. I laid this memo aside.

A week or two later I picked it up again to read it carefully, noting the way funds were distributed. The well-connected were grabbing the money for *their* projects. Most of the trails got not a penny. Here is a portion of the memo from Gary Werner, executive director of PNTS. The analysis follows.

FISCAL YEAR 2015 LAND AND WATER CONSERVATION FUNDING APPROPRIATED FOR THE NATIONAL TRAILS SYSTEM

The nearly $28 million of LWCF money included in the FY 2015 Cromnibus Appropriations Bill will fund just under half of the land acquisition projects included in the FY 2015 National Trails System Collaborative Landscape Planning (CLP) proposal for acquisition by the Bureau of Land Management, National Park Service, U.S. Forest Service and U.S. Fish and Wildlife Service. *This is by far the largest amount of LWCF money appropriated for National Trails System acquisition projects in a single year in well over a decade* [italics mine]. The money will fund important land purchases along 12 national scenic and historic trails—more trails than have ever been provided with LWCF funding in a single year's appropriation.

This Funding for National Trails System
LWCF Projects is included in the Cromnibus
Appropriations Bill for FY 2015:

Bureau of Land Management:

Pacific Crest National Scenic Trail in California
$950,000

Nez Perce National Historic Trail in Idaho
$3,000,000

Lewis and Clark National Historic Trail in
Montana $1,032,000

Sandy River / Oregon National Historic Trail in
Oregon $1,000,000

Pacific Crest National Scenic Trail in Oregon
$542,000

U.S. Fish and Wildlife Service:

Captain John Smith Chesapeake NHT in Virginia
$2,000,000

National Park Service:

Ala Kahakai National Historic Trail – Hawaii
$2,000,000

Appalachian National Scenic Trail – New
Hampshire $2,251,000

Appalachian National Scenic Trail – Vermont
$533,000

Captain John Smith Chesapeake NHT – Virginia
$4,000,000

Ice Age National Scenic Trail – Wisconsin
$1,664,000

New England National Scenic Trail –
Massachusetts $247,000

North Country National Scenic Trail – Michigan
$519,000

U.S. Forest Service:

Pacific Crest National Scenic Trail in California
$1,265,000

Pacific Crest National Scenic Trail in Washington
$1,320,000

Appalachian National Scenic Trail – Tennessee
$330,000

Pacific Northwest National Scenic Trail –
Washington $2,700,000

Old Spanish National Historic Trail – Miranda
Canyon NM $2,600,000

Total $27,953,000

Please share this information with other activists
in your organization and urge them to join you in
thanking the Appropriators and the Congressional
champions for your trail who helped secure this
LWCF funding.

Thanks for your essential help!

Gary Werner
Partnership for the National Trails System

In building a wilderness footpath through the woods
or across a desert or up on a ridge, the must-have is a
treadway. If, after a day of walking, you pass a view of
someone's backyard or if you come up to a paved road by

walking along the fence line of a gasoline station, I say, "Get over it." This is a price worth paying. But if you read a sign that says TRAIL CLOSED. PRIVATE PROPERTY, your hike is over.

Today you might hear a commercial aircraft 30,000 feet over your head or perhaps a diesel truck running through its gears two miles away—not just that clap of thunder in the distance, a Steller's jay in a ponderosa pine, or the sharp call of a pileated woodpecker. We are stuck with civilization ... but that's not all bad! We take for granted hot and cold running water, antibiotics, MRIs, museums, sports stadiums, public boat ramps, lifeguards on beaches, companies that publish magazines and books, and an army to defend our national borders. We are well into the second millennium and it's not all bad!

Furthermore, while I would love to find pure wilderness in all directions on my hikes, not everyone is such a purist. Most people probably wouldn't get annoyed by a tire track, a fence (even with a stile over it), or cars on a distant highway, even if I do. So while hikers have opinions about the distance between water sources, the grade of a trail, or whether a foot bridge has a railing, everyone needs the treadway.

In Werner's memo just referred to, look at the National Scenic Trails only. The Appalachian Trail, which possesses its treadway from Springer Mountain to Mount Katahdin, from end-to-end, received money from three sources:

From:		
National Park Service	$2,251,000	
National Park Service	$ 533,000	
U.S. Forest Service	$ 330,000	
Total	$3,114,000	

Conclusion: There are 11 trails within the National Scenic Trails System. The one footpath with a secure treadway sucked up 25% of the Land and Water Conservation Fund's foot trails allocation for "viewshed" acquisition and other reasons not as critical as buying treadway.

The Pacific Crest Trail can be hiked from Campo on the Mexican border, 2,650 miles to the Canadian border. Their problem: about 10% of their treadway is not secure for posterity. The trail could be closed—of huge concern for the 1,000 plus hikers who currently thru-hike it. It's even of concern for over a million hikers who just set foot on this fabulous trail each year. Mind you, this "not secure" statistic is not located in just one stretch of trail for the PCT or any of the other National Scenic Trails. The gaps break the trails in hundreds of places.

From the Werner memo, here is the LWCF allocation for the Pacific Crest Trail:

From: Bureau of Land Management	$ 950,000
Bureau of Land Management	$ 542,000
U.S. Forest Service	$1,265,000
U.S. Forest Service	$1,320,000
Total	$3,077,000

Conclusion: Of the 11 trails in the National Trails System, the Pacific Crest Trail also took 25% of the total foot trail allocation. So the one complete trail and the one almost complete trail grabbed half the funds available to these 11 trails.

National Historic Trails identify, promote and preserve the history of trails that played a significant and often dramatic role in the unfolding of our country's development. There are 19. But they don't have to be continuous. The prior users weren't seeking scenic beauty; they were seeking a way through. Unlike a footpath, most paths were marked by the ruts of wagon wheels ... in as much flat, open, well-drained land as the migrants could find.

In recognition of this history, I look for roadside panels and usually stop to read every word. Today the challenges facing these Historic Trails don't compare with the continuity problems confronting a footpath. Recognition of these trails doesn't have the urgency that continuity poses. Nevertheless, compare the money allocated to Historic Trails and Scenic Trails (footpaths):

    Historic Trails $15,632,000
    Scenic Trails $12,321,000

Before we leave the subject of Historic Trails, note that the Captain John Smith Chesapeake National Historic Trail gobbled up over 38.4% of the Historic Trails total. Captain John Smith mostly went from point to point in Chesapeake Bay by boat. What's behind this distortion? See below.

So we find that three trails of the 30 in the National Trails System received 43% of the $28 million. Ten got the rest; 17 got nothing. This is part of a pattern of inequities. The PNTS isn't doing its job and 17 trail clubs that formed to promote their trail are sitting on their hands. This LWCF appropriation of $28 million is not an everyday affair. It was acclaimed by trail leaders as a huge score. For three trails, yes. Most of the other 27 trails got little or nothing.

Here is a summary of what we have said:

1. Congress is not doing its job, either; they approved this lopsided allocation.

2. Our National Scenic Trails are divided, where two well-organized trail clubs are scooping up the attention and money and widening the gap between the haves and the have-nots. (I have added the Pacific Crest Trail to the A.T.) The nine have-nots are scrambling for crumbs. Among the 19 Historic Trails, one grabbed 38.4% of the dollars that should have been distributed among all. If Congress doesn't break this monopoly by supporting all more equally, we will forever have nine runts in one litter and 18 in the other.

3. One well-positioned, politically influential person can greatly affect results disproportionately. That's the reason huge sums were advanced for the Captain John Smith Chesapeake National Historic Trail. Every part of this bay is navigable; no right-of-way had to be purchased. At least $5 million of the $6 million was inappropriately approved by a Congress not doing its job. It's called "pork."

4. The figures show human nature at work. Those with influence got more than their share. Leadership that's asleep represents trails that suffer.

5. The PNTS is the organization that should not have let this happen.

In retrospect, the trails leadership, of which I am one, has failed in another way. Back in the beginning, in October 1968, after the trails act was signed into law, trail clubs that were created to support each of our iconic trails had the task of deciding whether or not they wanted the "National Scenic Trail (NST)" designation attached to their trail—as in, not just the "Florida Trail," but the "Florida National Scenic Trail."

Only the Long Trail in Vermont said "Thanks, but no thanks." I remember the Florida Trail Association Board of Directors' discussions as to what the NST designation meant and whether or not we wanted it. In the end we took the title. I should have been smart enough to see this mistake. Instead, I said nothing. I buy, sell and broker vacant Florida land for a living. I can't believe I didn't speak out in those days. We should have negotiated. We should have said, "We want what the A.T. received, sufficient sums to buy 300 miles of Florida rights-of-way. And we want eminent domain. Otherwise, count us out."

The task of acquiring treadway for a footpath has advantages to offer a federal agency over acquiring rights-of-way for a road. We don't need to have all the money in the bank before starting to buy a corridor. A road, a power line, or a gas project, for example, must get to work on their project. The public is waiting. The National Park Service, on the other hand, took more than 30 years to acquire the A.T. corridor. Utility lines must go where the people are. We want to build a foot trail where the people are not. Finally, a foot trail is more pleasing if it meanders; it can go around stuff. A road, railroad, or gas line is most efficient if it runs straight, so these corridors plow through many dwellings—even neighborhoods— toward their destinations.

3

Why We Need an Oversight Hearing Now

Today, many more people are hiking and backpacking. American needs more trails. And the system is growing without direction, either from Congress or anyone else. Yet we are told everything is okay. A "system" that needed tweaking within 10 years of passage of the Trails Act of 1968 has been unsupervised by Congress since 1978. It shows.

A list of possible additions to the National Trails System was given in the '68 and '78 act as trails to be studied. Some trails were selected after the studies were complete and some were not. It should not be assumed that this selection process was perfect. Some not selected might deserve a second review. One or two selected should be run through the process again; I doubt they would qualify. The act's sponsor in Congress with political influence has died. These trails should stand on their own merits, or not.

What we are seeing after 42 years is organic growth, the kind of healthy growth we see in the private sector that allows for enterprises to fail, to be bought out, or to succeed beyond our imagination. In a trails system, there needs to be more equality imposed by government agencies and by the Partnership for the National Trails System. Instead, "the rich get richer and the poor get poorer." This has been going on for years and is now egregious. The PNTS's listing of dollar requests from Congress in 2020 illustrates this point:

On February 6, 2020, the Partnership for the National Trails System requested that the House of Representatives, Committee on Appropriations, Subcommittee on Interior, Environment and Related Agencies appropriate the $17.640 million from the Land and Water Conservation Fund for National Scenic Trails land acquisition as follows:

$5.6 million – Pacific Crest National Scenic Trail (OR)
  – $5 million to Shasta-Trinity National Forest (CA) for Phase III of the Trinity Divide project (5,600 acres) which includes or is adjacent to portions of the Pacific Crest Trail in Northern California. Previous LWCF appropriations over three years ensured the completion of the first two phases of Trinity Divide in 2019. (FS)
  – $600,000 for trail and resource protection within the Cascade Siskiyou National Monument in southern Oregon. (BLM)

$5.45 M – Appalachian National Scenic Trail (NC, TN, VA, VT)
  – To acquire four national forests in four states to protect miles of several trout streams, relocate trail segments, preserve trail viewsheds, and provide habitat for rare birds and ecological connectivity and watershed protection near or adjacent to the Appalachian Trail. One parcel in NC is also within the viewshed of the Overmountain Victory National Historic Trail. (FS)

$3.5 M – Ice Age National Scenic Trail (WI)
 – To help acquire three parcels totaling 400 acres within the Cross Plains Unit of the Ice Age National Scientific Reserve in Dane County. (NPS)

$2.8 M – Continental Divide National Scenic Trail (CO)
 – To acquire land around the Muddy Pass area to facilitate relocation of the trail off a busy highway. (BLM)

$200,000 – Arizona National Scenic Trail (AZ)
 – To acquire an easement in Little Casa Blanca Canyon closing a gap in the trail and removing it from a dangerous road. (FS)

$90,000 – Florida National Scenic Trail (FL)
 – To fill trail gaps and provide connectivity between protected areas along the Withlacoochee River and adjacent to Suwannee River State Park. (FS)

$0 – Natchez Trace, New England, North Country, Pacific Northwest, Potomac Heritage National Scenic Trails

What is the one thing we need first for a trail? Of course, it is a continuous treadway with blazes. We can add "viewshed" acreage later. Even lean-tos and signs can come later. Treadway is the must-have.

Only one National Scenic Trail is continuous and secure through the efforts of the federal government. One is continuous, but only 90% secure. Again, the Arizona Trail and the Natchez Trace Trail are anomalies. Yet the A.T. and the PCT top the list for requested funds. The "big boys" are working the system. If the Partnership for the National Trails System is not strong enough to impose more equality, Congress should take charge so that treadway gets purchased as soon as possible for each trail.

This brings us to a corollary: Which two trails have the overcrowding problems? Of course, the Appalachian Trail and the Pacific Crest Trail. Here are their efforts at crowd control:

On the Appalachian Trail, long-distance hikers must now obtain permits, at no cost, to hike through state parks such as Baxter State Park in Maine. There are 14.4 miles of the A.T. in Baxter. It limits the number of A.T. Hiker Permit Cards to 3,150 hikers per season. If all available permit cards have been issued for the year, Katahdin will not be closed to A.T. hikers. However, "The Birches" long-distance hiker campsite will close for the year and A.T. hikers will then have two alternatives. They may make a reservation for the night before they summit at another campground in Baxter State Park. Or they may leave the park and spend the night in Millinocket before they summit in; they would then return the following morning as day-use visitors.

Hikers who plan to enter the park as day-use visitors via private vehicle are required to obtain a Day Use Parking Reservation (DUPR). During peak season (end of June through Labor Day) and on fall weekends, it may not be possible to obtain a camping or Day Use Parking Reservation for the desired date, meaning that hikers would need to delay their summit date.

In Great Smoky Mountains National Park, hikers who meet the definition of an A.T. thru-hiker (those who begin and end their hike at least 50 miles outside the park and only travel on the A.T. in the park) are eligible for a thru-hiker permit of $20 (valid for 38 days from the date issued, for a hike of up to eight days.) In the Smokies, regulations require that hikers stay in a shelter. While other backpackers must make reservations to use backcountry shelters, thru-hikers are exempt. From March 15 to June 15, four spaces at each A.T. shelter are reserved for thru-hikers. If the shelter is full, thru-hikers can tent close by. Only thru-hikers are allowed to tent next to shelters, so they are responsible for making room for those who have reservations in the shelters.

With respect to the Pacific Crest Trail, the U.S. Forest Service authorizes the Pacific Crest Trail Association to issue 50 permits per day for trips starting near Campos on the Mexican border; 1,400 permits for section hikers crossing the John Muir Trail may overlap with 600 permits for trips starting in the Southern Sierra, and 15 permits per day for trips starting near the Canadian border. Long-distance permits are only for hikers and horseback riders intending to travel 500 or more miles in a single continuous trip.

The PCT long-distance permit is an interagency permit for trips of 500 or more continuous miles that allows a hiker to travel through areas where local wilderness permits would otherwise be required.[6]

One thing we must accept is that hikers will seek out the most scenic places first. And they will do it when everyone else has the opportunity to do it … on three-day weekends. The old-timers who insist on solitude will go on weekdays and off-season. Those are individual choices. What we must guard against is the decline and eventual destruction of the resource. Too many people walking a trail in rain will for sure degrade the trail. The simple and sensible answer is more trails. But preference for prime spots will forever be with us. We all want to see those places. An anecdote describes a problem that won't go away:

It was spring 2017 and I was hiking on the Appalachian Trail with North Carolina friend Dave Lippy. We had left our car at Tellico Gap and were on a gentle climb toward Wesser Fire Tower, when we caught up to a young woman putting on her pack. At first, I thought she was hiking alone … a sensitive issue. An older man appeared and joined her; it turned out to be her father. He said he would be with her for another week or so.

I chatted with her. I had a small video camera with me and when she seemed to open up, I asked if I could interview her for one of my websites, Hiking Trails for America. She obliged me. Her name was Samantha. She was from Ohio. I asked if she was familiar with the Buckeye Trail. She gave me a quizzical look and then said she had heard of it. She thought it was about 2,000 miles long.

I pointed out that the Appalachian Trail from North Georgia to Maine was only slightly longer than 2,000 miles. She had traveled from home a long way south to hike a trail of similar length. Her response was short and clear: "The majority of that trail was on roads." She thought "they ran out of money or people stopped hiking it because it wasn't in the woods."

Factoid: The Buckeye Trail Association says their trail is 1,444 miles long and that it is the longest circular trail in the country. Sadly, 55% to 60% of the trail requires some kind of road walk.

So, for several reasons our National Trails System is divided—the haves and the have-nots, those that qualify and those that don't—reason enough to request of Congress another oversight hearing.

Here are some key issues for such a hearing:

1. How can the struggling trails reach the stature of the Appalachian Trail and the Pacific Crest Trail?

2. Which National Scenic Trails, if any, should be removed from the list?

3. The Appalachian Trail, the Natchez Trace Trail and the Potomac Heritage Trail are "units" of the National Park Service. What advantage is that to these three trails? Should all of our National Scenic Trails be units of the National Park Service?

It is easy to see that without dramatic changes, the two lead trails will be mobbed and then degraded. Our other lightly used National Scenic Trails are ready and waiting, underutilized and most with strong volunteer crews available to maintain them. Completing them will be a bargain—the quickest and least expensive way to provide additional outdoor recreation for Americans.

But step back a minute and look at what we have. What is a National Scenic Trail, anyway?

The stimulus for a trails act was the need to save the Appalachian Trail. It had been a private enterprise created by hikers enamored with the idea of a footpath through the Appalachian Mountains. But popularity of the trail had built it up rapidly and it outgrew the ability of a hiking club to acquire rights-of-way. In Congress there was support for preservation of the trail in the east, but not much support west of the Mississippi. A system of national scenic trails was the brilliant solution. I don't know who gets the credit. In any case, the A.T. was the prototype. It was complete, it was proving popular, it had support not only from the A.T. Conference, but also from the Appalachian Mountain Club in Boston, smaller clubs up and down the East Coast and many other affiliated groups.

And there was a trail-in-waiting ready to be chosen the second National Scenic Trail, nicely balanced politically on the West Coast—the Pacific Crest Trail. These were the only two trails identified as acceptable in the 1968 trails act. We didn't need a definition of a National Scenic Trail; we had chosen two trails as models for the act.

Here is what they represented:

1. A footpath in undeveloped mountain scenery
2. The first trail chosen was over 2,000 miles and the second over 2,600 miles
3. Far from population centers
4. An active club promoting and maintaining each trail
5. Largely complete

Nevertheless, there was a definition of sorts in the act:

> "… extended trails so located as to provide for maximum outdoor recreation potential and for the conservation and enjoyment of the nationally significant scenic, historic, natural or cultural qualities of the areas through which such trails may pass."[7]

The first five trails selected by Congress to be National Scenic Trails fit both the prototype and the definition:

	Designated Miles	States
1. A.T.	2,190	ME, NH, VT, CT, NY, NJ, PA, MD, WV, VA, TN, NC
2. PCT	2,650	CA, OR, WA
3. CDT	3,100	MT, ID, WY, CO, NM
4. NCT	4,600	MI, MN, ND, NY, OH, PA, WI
5. IAT	1,000	WI

Three more trails, added later, also fit the five characteristics mentioned above.

	Designated Miles	States
1. PNTS	1,200	ID, MT, WA
2. FT	1,300	FL
3. AZ	800	AZ[8]

But what about the last three: the Natchez Trace Trail (NTT), the New England Trail (NET) and the Potomac Heritage (PHT). It is embarrassing to even write about the NTT. I drove out to see it last year. The Natchez Trace Parkway is 440 miles long. The trail was meant to follow the parkway. Just for the noise factor, the result of being too close to the parkway should disqualify this trail. In fact, you can often see the cars, as well. But the big insult is that the trail is only 60 miles long! And this 60-mile stretch is divided into five separate, discontinuous segments! Congress needs to toss this baby out with the bathwater. Lastly, it's in disrepair. Either no one is pushing the National Park Service to make boardwalk and sign repairs, or the National Park Service hasn't allocated the money. Where is the supporting club? Not enough people care.

A crushing final fact: The very day the Natchez Trace Trail was selected as a National Scenic Trail, the definition of a National Scenic Trail was reduced in a new subsection to read:

> The term "extended trails" means trails
> or trail segments, which total at least one
> hundred miles … in length.[9]

Congress chose this "100 miles" and then couldn't even see that modest commitment fulfilled.

The Potomac Heritage Trail is a disappointment of a different sort. The U.S. Department of the Interior's map titled "Potomac Heritage" does not identify what the words "Potomac" and "Heritage" refer to. Obviously, if Congress has identified it as a National Scenic Trail, it should read "Potomac Heritage Trail." But that would be incorrect, so they put no noun in the title of their brochure. In short, the Potomac Heritage National Scenic Trail, one of 11, is a hodgepodge. About 25% of it is a bicycle path only. Part of it is the very popular and heavily used paved stretch opposite the Capitol and the Lincoln Memorial and the Washington Monument, opposite the array of government buildings and running adjacent to the George Washington Memorial Parkway on the west side of the Potomac River.

To cover themselves, the National Park Service says, in their brochure, that the "trail is an expanding network" that lets you retrace (history) by foot, bicycle, horse or boat. Their brochure calls it a "seamless" corridor. It is anything but. It certainly does not fit the description of a National Scenic Trail, based on the first five trails selected. There is a tiny isolated loop entirely within Prince William Forest Park. Otherwise, one can walk the Chesapeake and Ohio Canal towpath to Cumberland, MD, and the Allegheny Passage to Pittsburgh.

The only significant hiking trail is close to Pittsburgh, the Laurel Highlands Hiking Trail, running northeasterly from Ohiopyle, Pennsylvania, and outside the watershed of the Potomac. As the crow flies, it's about 50 miles southeast of Pittsburgh. This 70-mile-long trail runs northeast to southwest. It's 40 miles from the Potomac. It is "Potomac" mostly in the mind of an ad writer for the National Park Service. It is also a very fine footpath. Finally, hiking only. See Appendix 1 for more.

What should be done with this multiuse assortment of trails? It certainly shouldn't be listed with the first five hiking trails Congress chose to be called National Scenic Trails. Congress ultimately must answer this question. Yet again a reason for an oversight hearing of the 1968 and 1978 acts.

4

The Benefits of Walking ... and Hiking

Sometime between 1.5 and 2.5 million years ago, an anthropoid ape lifted his knuckles off the ground, straightened himself up and took a step. And then another. And the world was never the same. Once he was comfortable standing upright on two feet, he could walk. Behold, his hands were free. He could carry something in his arms. His opposable thumbs were refined over time to better grasp what he wanted to carry.

The DNA of a chimpanzee and that of a Homo sapiens is between 93.8 and 98.8% the same. No other living mammal has DNA so similar to ours. We may not know the exact route we took, but it is clear that the first thing we did was walk. It is not surprising that walking is good for us today. For men, in particular, walking to find meat had to be extensive. All of it was in nature. Call it hiking. In fact, I like the definition of hiking in *In Praise of Walking*, by Shane O'Mara: "What is hiking but walking in nature, for leisure and for exercise." Is it any wonder we respond to a walk in the woods? If we are urbanites and unfamiliar with our wooded surroundings, is it any wonder that we are apprehensive? Maybe we have been told that the largest animal we might see is a raccoon, but that may not calm our fears. There was a time long ago, when walking in nature, that we could have been killed and eaten. Nevertheless, it is what we know deep within us.

Is it any wonder that we like a bubbling fountain in our front yard? Camping by a babbling brook would have meant good water. Is it any wonder we like camping on the beach? The seas were full of fish once upon a time. Any wonder that children like to mess around a campfire today?

The Egyptian pyramids are less than 5,000 years old. I'm talking about a past that was perhaps 50 times further back in time than these pyramids. We were built to walk in nature, to respond to the sound of stillness, to redolent duff when wet, to the awe of the heavens without man-made light. Nothing I can think of can compare to hiking as passive activity we respond to and that we were designed over time to be part of. It might be the ideal activity to complete our lifestyle.

What other physical activity could we have performed over and over again, over the millennia, that would be more appropriate to resurrect than hiking to ensure a healthy body today?

Is swimming a possibility? Unlikely. Suitable water free from crocodiles would be hard to find in Africa. Running? Watch animals in the wild. They must run well to escape capture. But they don't run much. They walk a lot.

Fighting is the only other physical thing we still have in common with our past. But like running, it was sporadic. Peace reigned most days. This walking continued almost to the present. We have been told men should walk 18,000 steps a day because Amish men walk that much on their non-mechanized farms. After mustering out of the Civil War, most men walked home, however far that may have been. So if we want physical activity that inures to the benefit of us all, it's hiking in nature. I loved tennis while I played. I loved the competition and coming home exhausted for a shower, but hiking in nature is part of you and me like nothing else.

Just standing in nature is good for us. I remember years ago, en route to Tokyo, deciding to stay in a bona fide Japanese hotel. The hotel backed up to a private property. Between the property lines of the house and the hotel was a Japanese garden, formal and green, compact yet complete. Before sunrise I watched the owner standing in the middle of his garden, silent and still. I thought how fortunate he was to have a garden.

Running through nature ought to be beneficial; chatting with friends while on a nature path is better than a street, but hiking, best alone—with one or two others, if you prefer—remains in our DNA, the best form of exercise.

Do you have emotional issues on your mind, spiritual issues, mental issues, physical issues? Imagine back a million years. Seek out a hiking trail and take a walk for an hour ... better, for a day, even a week, a month if possible. Let the past eons help you with the present. John Muir said, "Climb the mountains and get their good tidings. Nature's peace will flow into you as sunshine flows into trees. The winds will blow their own freshness into you, and the storms their energy, while cares will drop off like autumn leaves."[10]

Recently we have discovered one more very pragmatic reason to support hiking trails. The solution to a problem has been in front of us for a while.

Instead of walking home, a U.S. soldier returning from Afghanistan, Iraq, or Syria could find himself at Bagram Air Base in Afghanistan on one day, Ramstein Air Base in Germany on the next and then in his mother's kitchen, watching her prepare his favorite meal while munitions still explode in his head. PTSD, post-traumatic stress disorder, was the result for many. Such travel arrangements replaced a troop ship leaving Europe for a four-week journey across the Atlantic, valuable down time for him to share with war buddies, precious time to talk out with fellow warriors the nightmares they shared.

At first, efforts to deal with PTSD came in from all over the place. Lots of ideas were simply wasted energy. Somehow, somewhere, some soldiers started taking backpacking trips together. The results were immediately impressive. UC Berkeley psychology professor Dacher Keltner has said, "Time outdoors changes people's nervous systems. It is as effective as any PTSD intervention we have."[11] These soldier-backpackers find themselves in a physically demanding, secure, natural environment with no distractions, in the company of warriors like themselves. In fact, in no time these events acquired the appropriate title of Warrior Hikes. Hikers immediately understood the value of our long trails for this purpose. By the way, a Warrior Hike's criteria is that a trail be at least 1,200 miles long. Our Florida Trail has sponsored many of these hikes.

Of course, the benefits of hiking are there for everyone. We all have a sense of what they are. But I am staring at a list and am annoyed by the way these statements present "facts" to a tenth of a degree: "... hiking for 20 minutes in nature helps to decrease your heart rate by 6.8%." The statement is pretentious. If it only "helps," something else is helping. What else? Does the hike provide most of the benefit or only 1/10 of it? We aren't told. Here is another example: "... hiking can result in up to a 50% improvement in creative and reasonable thinking." It "can," but what are the odds it will do anything of the sort? Does "up to ... 50%" mean from 0 to 50% or 40 to 50%? I have no idea. Hiking makes people feel better and actually be better in a wide range of ways.

Here is a list of benefits that pop up regularly. I have seen these benefits myself. (I have left off percentiles to a tenth of a degree.)

1. Hiking in nature improves creative thinking.

2. Hiking in nature assists in maintaining mental health.

3. Hiking in nature reduces stress significantly.

4. Hiking in nature lowers your heart rate and blood pressure.

5. Hiking helps you burn calories.

6. Hiking aids in strengthening your immune system.

7. It helps reduce symptoms of arthritis.

8. It helps your lungs function more efficiently.

9. Hiking in nature improves a positive attitude, which reduces anxiety and abates depression.

10. Hiking increases bone density.

11. Obviously, hiking greatly increases the health and strength of your legs, which in turn strengthens your entire body.

12. Such exercise lowers the risk of colon and breast cancer and probably other cancers as well.

13. Hiking will help you fall asleep and will enable you to sleep better.

There is a difference between taking a walk and going for a hike in the woods. If you don't believe me, try the hike. Researchers at Stanford University have spent years studying the effects of hiking on the psyche.

Some advice:

1. Exposure to nature doesn't have to mean a multi-day expedition.

2. Nature and rigorous movement go together. Get both.

3. Tranquility in nature increases serotonin levels that fight both depression and anxiety.

4. The sights, sounds and smells of nature are known to calm a busy mind.

5. Walking on flat terrain requires only a routine rhythm. A footpath requires the mind to coordinate the body with every uneven step, making much more complete use of muscles. Balance and stability get a workout.

6. Want to socialize? Bring friends and share the experience.

7. Wear yourself out on the trail.

8. Take a compass; leave your phone behind.

These are the health benefits for you; however, hiking benefits society as well. It's democratic, open to everyone. One's economic level, the diversity of one's race or religion, one's age—none of these matter. It would help if you owned a pair of sneakers. If you want to hike in the snow or over wet ground, it would help to own a pair of hiking boots. It would help, but it's not essential. If your child is three, your hike may terminate in 100 yards. My twins took an overnight hike when they were five. Grandma Gatewood hiked from Georgia to Maine when she was 67, back in 1955. She did it two more times before 1963, when she retired from hiking at age 75.[12]

It's also democratic because it costs little to take up hiking. You can purchase a backpack; Grandma Gatewood slung a sack over one shoulder. You should be able to find lightweight everything in your own pantry or garage, but Recreational Equipment, Inc., would be happy to see you.

Trails are inexpensive to maintain because of the trail culture that exists. Volunteers maintain our iconic trails through local hiking clubs. The National Park Service, part of the Department of the Interior, helps with costs of our 11 National Scenic Trails, but those trails would remain open and useable if government dollars and personnel disappeared. Older hikers enjoy getting outside to do clearing work.

There is one significant one-time expense. Private citizens can't buy rights-of-way. They don't have the money and they also don't have the authority. Back in 1968 when Congress elected to create a National Trails System, it provided eminent domain for the Appalachian Trail to purchase 700 miles of the 2,190-mile trail. This job took over 30 years, yet the task got done.

5

Volunteer Trail Maintenance, Federal Highway Acquisitions, and the Use of Eminent Domain

In an effort to learn more about the history of acquiring the entire Appalachian Trail right-of-way, I flew to Washington to speak to key people in the Appalachian Trail Conservancy (ATC), bureaucrats in the U.S. Forest Service and the National Park Service and others familiar with this history. These included, among others, Don King, Pam Underhill, Jim Snow, Chuck Sloan. and Paul Pritchard. The conclusions I drew from my conversations and the data collected are my own.

Congress came to the aid of the Appalachian Trail with money and eminent domain when the A.T. was 66% complete. The National Trails System Act of 1968 and the amendment that followed it in the '78 act represent a Congressional effort to create a trails system for America. Since then, Congress has hardly lifted a finger. When benefits are weighed against cost and we see the opportunity that the Congress has failed to recognize and support, it should bring us to tears.

Today the Pacific Crest Trail is 90% secure and 100% continuous, but Congress has not stepped up to do for the PCT what it did for the A.T.

Today the Florida Trail is 73% complete, requiring 300 miles of paved road walks, but Congress has not stepped up to provide for the nation the only winter footpath free of snow.

Today the 3,100-mile Continental Divide Trail is 76% complete, but it receives a fraction of the hikers who set off on the A.T., a trail that Congress completed when it was only 66% secure.

Other chapters in this book support the claim that trails are the bargain of a lifetime. Government, step up and buy the rights-of-way! Older citizens who no longer want to hike the length of these trails will maintain them. I'm not making this up. See the two charts that follow, for 2019. These are real numbers assiduously collected by the clubs, courtesy of the PNTS

2019 Trail Organization(s)	Active Volunteers	Volunteer Hours	Value of Volunteer Hours	Private Contributions
Ala Kahakai Trail Association and E Mau Nā Ala Hele	423	423	$10,757	$8,725
Anza Trail Foundation and partners	276	11,133	$283,112	$90,350
Appalachian Trail Conservancy	5,867	210,923	$5,363,772	$7,579,015
Arizona Trail Association	2,271	22,389	$569,352	$736,500
Chesapeake Conservancy and partners	-	-	-	$170,000
Connecticut Forest & Park Association and Appalachian Mountain Club	478	4,249	$108,052	$36,000
Continental Divide Trail Coalition and partners	420	42,000	$1,068,060	$621,564
El Camino Real de los Tejas NHT Association	55	8,860	$225,310	$70,543
El Camino Real de Tierra Adentro Trail Association	19	980	$24,921	$2,975
Florida Trail Association	623	23,379	$594,528	$521,627
Ice Age Trail Alliance	2,376	82,880	$2,107,638	$1,141,000
Iditarod Historic Trail Alliance	1,800	15,000	$381,450	$8,994
Lewis and Clark Trail Heritage Foundation, Lewis and Clark Trust, Inc., and partners	215	70,378	$1,789,713	$115,050
Mormon Trails Association and partners	-	-	-	$25

2019 Trail Organization(s)	Active Volunteers	Volunteer Hours	Value of Volunteer Hours	Private Contributions
Natchez Trace Parkway Association	60	1,200	$30,516	$6,700
National Pony Express Association	1.260	32,812	$834,409	$8,575
National Washington-Rochambeau Revolutionary Route NHT Association, Inc. (W3R-US)	218	11,714	$297,887	$8,290
Nez Perce Trail Foundation	7	7,500	$190,725	$1,500
North Country Trail Association	1,058	83,300	$2,118,319	$654,300
Old Spanish Trail Association	449	27,610	$702,122	$12,000
Oregon-California Trails Association	400	104,806	$2,665,217	$713,350
Overmountain Victory Trail Association	400	30,363	$772,131	$96,156
Pacific Crest Trail Association	2,038	106,444	$2,706,871	$3,119,796
Pacific Northwest Trail Association	221	19,620	$498,937	$105,813
Potomac Heritage Trail Association	15	4,000	$101,720	$30,000
Santa Fe Trail Association	1,098	72,546	$1,844,845	$64,250
Trail of Tears Association	177	25,158	$621,151	$11,700
Totals (pg 46 and 47)	**22,224**	**997,162**	**$25,357,830**	**$15,934,798**

Notes: Value of volunteer time calculated using the national 2018 value of volunteer time ($25.43/hour) by the Independent Sector. We will update the value of volunteer hours when the 2019 per hour value is announced by the Independent Sector. Some, but not all trail organizations include federal reimbursement rates for miles driven for volunteer work as part of their private contributions. Volunteer Stewardship activities include, but are not limited to: trail building and maintenance, outreach event development, youth engagement, public education, development of interpretive materials and sites, removal of invasive species, habitat restoration, land protection, historic research, reenactments, archaeological studies and community partnership development.

Partnership for the National Trails System

Contributions Sustaining the National Scenic and Historic Trails Made by Partner Trail Organizations 2019

Year	Volunteer Hours	Estimated Value of Volunteer Labor	Financial Contributions	Total $ Value
1995	369,941	$4,262,093	$2,754,934	$7,017,027
1996	473,066	$4,467,794	$4,071,409	$8,529,203
1997	439,299	$5,686,028	$4,243,943	$9,929,971
1998	498,702	$6,909,157	$4,403,802	$11,312,959
1999	553,905	$7,422,326	$5,780,340	$13,202,666
2000	593,392	$8,799,993	$6,638,313	$15,438,306
2001	621,615	$9,566,652	$6,652,079	$16,218,731
2002	662,429	$10,631,985	$6,850,214	$17,482,199
2003	648,548	$10,726,994	$6,997,803	$17,724,797
2004	668,996	$11,801,091	$6,449,719	$18,250,810
2005	723,191	$13,046,366	$7,275,556	$20,321,922
2006	687,904	$12,409,472	$7,934,074	$20,343,546
2007	720,935	$13,540,396	$8,064,293	$21,604,689
2008	771,993	$15,631,643	$9,108,338	$24,739,981
2009	907,380	$18,601,296	$8,823,248	$27,424,544
2010	1,115,559	$24,366,484	$12,486,240	$36,852,724
2011	1,141,866	$24,390,258	$8,714,610	$33,104,868
2012	1,185,375	$26,244,202	$7,509,777	$33,753,979
2013	1,144,407	$25,337,171	$10,685,751	$36,022,922
2014	1,053,896	$23,765,355	$10,836,694	$34,602,049
2015	1,073,026	$24,754,710	$12,396,728	$37,151,438
2016	1,029,569	$24,256,645	$13,184,886	$37,441,531
2017	1,046,194	$25,796,531	$14,485,936	$40,282,467
2018	978,034	$24,871,405	$14,489,472	$39,360,877
2019	997,162	$25,357,830	$15,934,798	$41,292,628
Total	**20,106,384**	**$402,643,877**	**$216,772,957**	**$619,416,834**

The 1995 and 1996 totals represent contributions from 20 organizations for 20 national scenic and historic trails while the 1997–2001 totals represent the contributions of 22 organizations for those trails and the 2002–2005 totals represent the contributions of 24 organizations for 21 national scenic and historic trails. The 2006 and 2007 totals are the contributions of 23 organizations for 20 national scenic and historic trails. The 2009 and 2010 totals include the contributions for four new national scenic and historic trails authorized by Congress in 2009. (Dollar values are not adjusted for inflation.)

In 2018 the Outdoor Foundation said there were 44.9 million hikers who took 14 or more outings a year. In 2020 they said there were 47.9 million hikers in America.[13] These are enormous numbers. Appropriate government employees need to see these important statistics.

In just the DOT examples that follow, we see clearly that government agencies across America are acquiring property on a daily basis, much of it by eminent domain. Again, the authority to do so is right there in the Bill of Rights. Every town in America can appropriate eminent domain.

Here is what we say about eminent domain in Florida:

Sec 2019 FL Statutes 166.401 and 166.411

Florida Statutes 166.401
Right of eminent domain; procedure;
compliance with limitations.—

1. All municipalities in the state may exercise the right and power of eminent domain; that is, the right to appropriate property within the state, except state or federal property, for the uses or purposes authorized pursuant to this part. The absolute fee simple title to all property so taken and acquired shall vest in such municipal corporation unless the municipality seeks to condemn a particular right or estate in such property.

2. Each municipality is further authorized to exercise the eminent domain power granted to the Department of Transportation in s. 337.27(1) and the transportation corridor protection provisions of s. 337.273.

3. The local governing body of a municipality may not exercise its power of eminent domain unless the governing body adopts a resolution authorizing the acquisition of a property, real or personal, by eminent domain for any municipal use or purpose designated in such resolution.

4. Each municipality shall strictly comply with the limitations set forth in ss. 73.013 and 73.014.

History.—s. 1, ch. 73-129; s. 5, ch. 88-168; s. 18, ch. 90-227; s. 63, ch. 99-385; s. 13, ch. 2006-11.

166.411   Eminent domain; uses or purposes.—
Subject to the limitations set forth in ss. 73.013 and 73.014, municipalities are authorized to exercise the power of eminent domain for the following uses or purposes:

1. For the proper and efficient carrying into effect of any proposed scheme or plan of drainage, ditching, grading, filling, or other public improvement deemed necessary or expedient for the preservation of the public health, or for other good reason connected in anywise with the public welfare or the interests of the municipality and the people thereof;

2. Over railroads, traction and streetcar lines, telephone and telegraph lines, all public and private streets and highways, drainage districts, bridge districts, school districts, or any other public or private lands whatsoever necessary to enable the accomplishment of purposes listed in s. 180.06;

3. For streets, lanes, alleys, and ways;

4. For public parks, squares, and grounds;

5. For drainage, for raising or filling in land in order to promote sanitation and healthfulness, and for the taking of easements for the drainage of the land of one person over and through the land of another;

6. For reclaiming and filling when lands are low and wet, or overflowed altogether or at times, or entirely or partly;

7. For the use of water pipes and for sewerage and drainage purposes;

8. For laying wires and conduits underground; and

9. For city buildings, waterworks, ponds, and other municipal purposes which shall be coextensive with the powers of the municipality exercising the right of eminent domain.

History.—s. 1, ch. 73-129; ss. 1, 2, ch. 2001-77; s. 4, ch. 2005-3; s. 14, ch. 2006-11.

That's just for municipalities. The state and federal government also have eminent domain. Many in the hiking community believe that eminent domain is not available for trails. How did this happen? This view is, as far as I can tell, universally accepted within the leadership of the Partnership of the National Trails System. How surprising when the first National Scenic Trail is the only continuous National Scenic Trail out of the 11 and continuous only because Congress provided eminent domain to ensure its continuity. We were handed an archetype by Congress, a template for national trails, and we let a few cattlemen in the West intimidate us. Hikers are very nice people, so they have backed up against a wall and allowed themselves to think that the possible is impossible. Congress placed eminent domain in the '68 act because they knew the A.T. needed it.

The only trail leaders I know of who are not committed to rejecting eminent domain to complete our National Scenic Trails are the board members of Hiking Trails for America, which was founded in 2013 for the sole purpose of closing the gaps in the National Scenic Trails. When the executive director of the Appalachian Trail Conservancy retired, I invited him to serve on the board of HTA; but in a couple of years he resigned, citing concerns over our expressed support for eminent domain in closing the gaps in our National Scenic Trails—this, in spite of the fact that his trail, the A.T., the only trail of the 11 to be continuous, *had been made so by the judicious use of eminent domain by Congress!*

Let's think for a moment about the idea of rejecting the use of eminent domain to complete any of the corridors of our National Scenic Trails. It's helpful to look at Congress and the A.T. experience from 1978 until about 2010.

Of the 700 miles the National Park Service acquired for the A.T. to be complete and continuous from Maine to Georgia, 2,550 parcels needed to be purchased. Of those, about 400 made use of eminent domain. Of those, about 100 were adversarial. Most of the rest had title issues that needed to be settled so that the government knew who was getting money for the taking and how much each party was being paid. From government numbers, 15.7% of the total takings required eminent domain. Please keep that number handy.

With a percentage like that, how can anyone say that they will complete our National Scenic Trails without the use of eminent domain?

The corridors of the 10 National Scenic Trails total 16,000 miles. The gaps today in these trails, in spite of the best efforts over many years to find a way through, total 4,074 miles. In other words, 25% of our National Scenic Trails are in gaps in spite of the fact that trails leadership has been seeking to close these gaps actively for decades. In spite of this depressing statistic, the trails leadership will tell you they intend to close our trail gaps without eminent domain.

Companies that build gas lines, power lines, railroads, water and sewer lines and roads need a continuous corridor. What experiences, I wondered, have any of these had in negotiating rights-of-way without eminent domain? Very early on I found that they had eminent domain in their back pocket, before they began their first serious negotiation. Early on I thought the DOTs in each state would be the most helpful because they were the most active. New roads and the widening of roads are everyday occurrences.

If a state road is part of a federal highway, the state asks for federal money and the fed requires an accounting. By going after federal roads through states, we found all the data we needed. The data of these road acquisitions is available for each year. We chose 2019. In particular, we wanted the number of parcels acquired that year, the number of miles and whether or not eminent domain was required. We added the total number of parcels acquired across the country in all 50 states and the number of times eminent domain was used. It was used 16.5% of the time. Now, remember that the National Park Service needed eminent domain in 15.7% of its A.T. acquisitions. If we total the federal DOT acquisitions for 2019, of 32,598, and A.T. acquisitions over a 30-year period, of 2,550, we have 35,148 transactions, a huge sample for our purposes. Yet our trails leadership steadfastly maintains we will complete trails without it! The emperor has no clothes. The DOT data follows.

Federal Highway Administration
Parcels Acquired – 2019

State	Parcels Acquired	Parcels Acquired by Condemnation	Parcels Acquired by Administrative Settlement	Compensation - Total Costs
AK	260	10	63	3,816,278
AL	163	45	46	20,632,774
AR	0	0	0	0
AS	0	0	0	0
AZ	41	2	5	3,811,604
CA	828	51	488	60,059,517
CNMI	479	16	133	33,719,071
CO	0	0	0	0
CT	215	26	7	6,632,280
DC	3	0	0	41,231,644
DE	31	8	8	1,235,165

State	Parcels Acquired	Parcels Acquired by Condemnation	Parcels Acquired by Administrative Settlement	Compensation - Total Costs
FL	547	125	204	100,519,730
GA	1,753	281	169	197,141,086
GUAM	2	2	0	356,400
HI	7	1	0	1,094,959
IA	1,539	30	169	30,978,635
ID	161	2	54	442,796
IL	1,933	131	510	25,412,230
IN	740	74	146	62,574,107
KS	502	17	129	1,895,998
KY	387	96	161	34,071,932
LA	184	52	26	10,252,9995
MA	1,645	1,232	17	14,786,008
MD	720	704	66	2,515,731
ME	0	0	0	0
MI	499	1	22	21,703,321
MN	1,434	166	260	40,907,900
MO	726	19	231	9,222,136
MS	293	33	69	12,960,551
MT	401	1	88	10,456,272
NC	3,453	586	417	116,201,875
ND	196	1	4	1,247,718
NE	612	12	228	16,023,097
NH	68	2	9	4,223,203
NJ	0	0	0	0
NM	517	76	19	5,324,328
NV	0	0	0	0
NY	555	4	0	9,365,868
OH	1,807	210	466	35,657,898
OK	1,066	121	630	46,686,605
OR	353	9	30	9,962,298
PA	1,061	150	283	31,577,367
PR	46	45	1	1,673,108

State	Parcels Acquired	Parcels Acquired by Condemnation	Parcels Acquired by Administrative Settlement	Compensation - Total Costs
RI	67	62	0	184,218
SC	535	109	276	25,718,539
SD	578	0	100	4,197,827
TN	597	97	147	49,427,730
TX	2,628	524	422	378,299,477
USVI	18	0	0	540,335
UT	287	8	91	8,400,951
VA	679	118	362	57,780,145
VT	206	13	47	40,200
WA	663	21	178	92,566,799
WI	713	47	102	7,200,384
WV	218	30	34	37,314,955
WY	182	1	2	1,173,278
TOTAL	**32,598**	**5,371**	**6,919**	**$1,689,219,323**

https://www.fhwa.dot.gov/real_estate/uniform_act/stats/index.cfm#top

6

Utilities and Eminent Domain

We have discussed the National Park Service acquisition of 700 miles that was needed to complete a trail from Mount Katahdin to Springer Mountain. And we analyzed 32,598 recorded acquisitions by the federal Department of Transportation. What about utilities? All of them need eminent domain, particularly when acquiring a corridor. Getting accurate data from utilities is a huge problem. They are not required to report real estate transactions anywhere. The data is buried in thousands of files for each major utility. Besides, they consider it proprietary and are quick to tell you so. They don't want to share the details of their real estate transactions.

However, Atlantic Coast Pipeline was attempting to acquire right-of-way to extend a natural gas line through West Virginia, Virginia and North Carolina. They were doing just fine until they got to the Appalachian Mountains—specifically, the Appalachian Trail. The Appalachian Trail Conservancy leadership advised them that they were not granting them permission to cross the trail. This event made big news; I saw it mentioned in various publications several times. My first reaction was, Of course not. I pictured a 24-inch pipe, several feet above ground, held in place by reinforced concrete stanchions, winding its way uphill through the Appalachian forest and blocking the famous footpath.

Some source said that the pipeline would be six feet underground. I went to the Atlantic Coast Pipeline (ACP) website to see what I could learn. For one thing, Dominion Energy was behind the project; ACP was the contractor employed to build the line. Their website contained the name of a public relations executive named Aaron Ruby. I called him.

I got an earful from Ruby. Virtually everything I had been told was contradicted by what he said. I was surprised to learn that the closest above-ground part of the line would be a half a mile on either side of the trail. Instead of six feet underground, it would be 700 feet below the surface where it crossed the trail. I scratched my head. Why did the Appalachian Trail Conservancy object to the pipeline for many months, requiring ACP to file suit against the National Park Service, given these circumstances? Ruby told me there are already 200 crossings of the A.T. by utilities. What was so special about this one? Although the A.T. was the face of the lawsuit and brought enormous goodwill to the public debate about the validity of the suit and of the request to cross, the Southern Environmental Law Center, based in Atlanta, was funding the lawsuit. Ruby suggested that the ATC was a stalking horse. The Appalachian Trail is a household name, much admired and respected. It could be used in the same sentence with "motherhood" and "apple pie." Ruby spoke for Atlantic Coast Pipeline. To make up facts for a call like mine would make no sense; I could check everything, so I tended to believe what he said. Why would the Appalachian Trail Conservancy allow itself to be used in this way? I have no idea. I thought it was a huge mistake and I wrote the president to say so.

There is a secondary reason why it was a mistake, and it is every bit as important. Eventually the facts get out. The lawsuit, it turns out, in the first inning was all about who had jurisdiction to decide if ACP could cross the trail—the U.S. Forest Service or the National Park Service. That's not an A.T. issue. Every bit as important, when the Ruby facts emerged, the Appalachian Trail Conservancy looked unreasonable. Apparently, the Southern Environmental Law Center wants to halt the use of all nonrenewable energy, including natural gas. It will try to stop the construction of every gas line if it can. That may be a worthy objective. Or not. But it is not an issue over which the ATC should squander its good name. Its mission is to serve the purpose of hikers. Worse yet, many people, including outdoor lovers, will see hiking clubs as unreasonable in opposing relatively clean nonrenewable energy.

The ATC and the A.T. can weather this storm. The footpath is continuous from end-to-end and is secure for posterity. Every other National Scenic Trail has issues with continuity and permanency. Each trail needs as much favorable public image as it can get. It needs friends in every camp, and their efforts can't be seen as unreasonable.

But now let's look at the statistics Ruby provided. Up to the point where they abandoned the pipeline, Atlantic Coast Pipeline acquired 3,000 properties in their march east; 5% of their acquisitions needed eminent domain. Odd, you say. Why isn't it close to the 15% or 16% already mentioned? Ruby explained that a gas line (or sewer line or water line) is underground. The "taking" is easier for the property owner to live with. This line could cut across his pasture, across his front yard, as a matter of fact, and once the grass grows back, no one would know the line was there. As a result, it is easier for the property owner to see a win-win. No one can tell that the gas line comes through, and the property owner puts the funds in the bank. That, I believe, explains the difference between Ruby's 5% and the A.T./DOT percentages of 15–16%. If it does, we have an amazingly consistent set of statistics. People affected by road department takings and trail corridor takings can assume that 15–16% of the acquisitions will require eminent domain.

The hiking club leadership in America must look at this statistic. The view that the Pacific Crest Trail, the Ice Age Trail, the Florida Trail, the Continental Divide Trail and the North Country Trail—these longest of our National Scenic Trails with hundreds of miles of gaps— can be closed through "public and private partnerships" is a fantasy. It's dreaming the impossible dream.

The answer to completing these icons of outdoor recreation lies elsewhere. I want to point the reader in directions where solutions might be found.

7

The Special Problems
of Buying a Corridor

As we saw in the first six chapters, there are a whole host of reasons why government and many other entities would need eminent domain. But the acquisition of a corridor, for any use, is in a category by itself. If the entity with eminent domain authority needs a site, a parcel of a given size, and it can't have its first choice, it might find something similar nearby. But if the need is for a corridor, then its first purchase suddenly sets parameters for all the purchases that follow. Every acquisition must relate to the specifics of the alignment; each is driven by purchases that precede it in relation to the alignment.

Let's say a small town needs a fire station. Call each house a point. The locus of points determines that the ideal site is at Fifth and Main. But there are two banks, an office building and a gas station on these corners. The site selection committee should start looking down Fifth Avenue and down Main Street for vacant land. Coming off the intersection will also reduce the price. One hundred yards or so should not greatly alter how the station functions.

A corridor imposes far more restrictions than the situation above. From the moment the first parcel is purchased, the acquiring party is locked into two properties, one on each side of it. Imagine trying to acquire those two parcels through negotiations. Let's say the two property owners know you need their property. What would you do if you were one of them? I know what I would do. I would raise my price. Now let's say the corridor in question needs to go through a field I own next door to my house, and I have plans for that field. One of my children wants to build a house there ... and my wife is thrilled with that idea. I would raise the price a lot. Instead, the taking authority can impose its will on me, but I will still have my day in court. A jury will hear just why I love that field so much and will be tasked with determining an appropriate award.

Why should a government have that taking right at all? Because the founders believed that a public need supersedes the need of one person. A few centuries ago, if the king wanted your land, he took it. Worse than that, in England, the birthplace of our legal system, nobles also seized land from commoners through intimidation and force. Remnants of these vast holdings still exist in Great Britain today. The power to take was replaced on this side of the Atlantic by the power to take, but with fair compensation—an enormous improvement.

Years ago, when money was more readily available from Congress through the U.S. Forest Service for the acquisition of trail rights-of-way, the USFS, in partnership with the Florida Trail Association (FTA), set out to buy several adjacent private parcels that lay within the alignment of the Florida Trail. Think "beads on a string." There may have been five of them. Over $2 million was spent on all but one of the parcels. The owner of the fifth parcel changed his mind and decided he didn't want to sell. And that is the way things remain to this day. Time and money were wasted buying the first four. When I questioned the U.S. Forest Service manager about the wisdom of buying those first parcels, he shrugged and said, "Well, we just have surplus land to sell." Spoken like someone who didn't have to put up the money.

If there is one private parcel sitting between two tracts in public ownership and it comes up for sale, buy it. Realize that we have over 4,000 miles of gaps in a National Trails System. But who would be improvident enough to put money into buying those beads on a string unless he knew he could buy them all and complete a continuous stretch of treadway? Not only must we fear an owner who decides he doesn't want to sell, we must contend with another inevitable event. One of the parcel owners hears that buying those beads on a string has begun; or if he's shrewd enough, he stalls after agreeing until the buying has begun, and then when the others have signed, he raises his price. Wiley Hicks, an eminent domain lawyer in Miami, said to me, "I always want my client to go last."

I remember moving to Miami in the late 1950s. The Boston department store, Jordan Marsh, had come to town a few years earlier, with a fine location on Biscayne Boulevard. I always wondered why, at the northwest corner of their huge building, there was a small cutout and a single-family home left standing on the boulevard. I entered the real estate business and eventually heard the story of the holdout. As Jordan Marsh was assembling a parcel big enough for parking plus their building, this party wouldn't sell. No eminent domain for department stores existed. Executives of the company had to decide whether they would walk away from their location, pay the seller's price—probably exorbitant—or build around this tiny parcel. They chose the latter. The small house has been there ever since, now no place for a home on such a busy street and too small for any commercial use. The owner probably regrets not making a deal. Sometimes there is not much difference between being smart and appearing greedy.

Of all the public uses for corridors, by far the most flexible when laying out the alignment is a footpath for hikers. Think of corridor uses: railroad, highway, canal, power line, water or sewer line, gas line, snowmobile trail, horse trail, bike trail, cross-country ski trail; what have I missed? Keep in mind, we want our hiking trails to be as remote as possible—one more huge advantage when locating a route. None of these is as flexible as a meandering footpath.

8

Conversations with an Eminent Domain Lawyer

It seems as if everyone today is angry at eminent domain. I am not sure why. Earlier this year I put a check in my bank account for $34,714.59, a partial payment on my share in a tract of Florida land. The state offered $4 per square foot. We countered with $11 per square foot. A year later we settled for $9 per square foot, about what it was worth. The state took our road frontage.

The frontage was on a two-lane road into the Jacksonville International Airport. As I write this, a four-lane divided highway into the airport is under construction, and the remaining land became a smaller parcel with the same amount of frontage. Some future user may or may not like that. The lineal feet of frontage for this parcel remains the same.

If the mood today over eminent domain existed in 1968, Congress would probably not have provided it for the A.T. in the National Trails System Act. It's been 42 years. By now this famous foot trail would have been broken into a hundred pieces.

As a property owner, my experiences with eminent domain have been acceptable. I have thought about the opposite opinion, that the taking is not acceptable.

Here are four reasons why property owners may resent this taking power.

- Governments, from cities to federal departments in Washington, DC, just like most of us, never have all the money they want. It's not surprising that when they need property and a "taking" is required, the pressure is on to offer the property owner less than fair market value. I can believe that most of the time, property owners are not experienced negotiators. They don't know how to look out for themselves; they might not even know how to assemble an experienced team to deal with the government and create a counteroffer. But no matter what number the property owners accept, in time, since all land values rise, the owners will be convinced that they sold too cheaply.

- Eminent domain has been abused in the past. Often under the rubric of urban blight, a city condemns property adjacent to the downtown core. It's undervalued because of its current use. The city then signs an agreement with a developer to convert the cleared land for some much more productive use—a high-rise office building, perhaps. The developer gets vacant land on which to construct an impressive, close-in income property. The city gets an attractive structure to add to the downtown core and the tax revenues that flow from that. The original property owner sees the transformation and realizes much later that what he or she received for the site is a pittance compared to its value after the transformation. The resentments are palpable.

- Frequently the taking includes not just a house, but a home. The home itself could be a family heirloom, a homesite spanning more than one generation and full of memories. At the emotional level, the reasons why the seller might not want to sell in this case are endless. The resentments are endless also.

- Governments are not naïve, not innocent. In their effort to acquire a property at the lowest possible price, they turn to strategies. I will mention two. (1) "Willing seller." On the surface, it would seem simple enough. But it could be code for something devious. In an assemblage of many parcels, the acquiring agency can pick off a few of the bargain properties scattered through a tract to be acquired. The other willing sellers are left to sit for a while. It could be years. The remaining property owners have no one else to sell to because it will be known that an assemblage is in progress and so there are no other buyers. Sell now, is the government implication, or we will buy it from you later for less. (2) Another strategy might be called "public and private partnerships." A large tract is privately owned. The owner may have long-term plans. But the government may also have long-term plans. When the private owner proceeds to seek approvals for a project, public needs surface in the approval process for the private owner. He or she learns that the county would like to meander a horseback riding trail as a circumferential route around this city and our private owner has land in the proposed route. The county will withhold approval for the owner's plans until the owner agrees to gift a needed corridor to the county for its share of the corridor just described. We could list dozens of reasons why the city, county, or state might like a parcel of land that the property owner can be required to gift in order to receive the approvals he or she needs.

- The Bill of Rights, part of our U.S. Constitution, addresses the subject of this entire chapter in a portion of one sentence. It's found in paragraph five and states as follows: "nor shall private property be taken for public use without just compensation."

From our perspective today, some can't see the reasoning in the minds of the founders for this statement, which most people would see as reasonable. The idea of a "taking" was not new. The government might have an important reason to take land belonging to someone, which most people could see as being reasonable. The critical part of the statement, then, becomes "just compensation."

Today some are inclined to say that the government ought not to have any right whatsoever to take a piece of private property. In the days of the founders, that wasn't the thought; receiving just compensation was the thought. Unfortunately, most of us are not reliably objective at all times. Given the opportunity, we will look out for our own interests first. Imagine a city land acquisition department. Imagine the city needs a park and thinks it doesn't have the money to pay a fair price for it. Hence, employees will be inclined to abuse their position, pay as little as possible for this property, and take advantage of the property owner in order to deliver the property to their boss at a good price. Today, what government agencies need to do is focus on the last phrase in this one sentence: "just compensation."

I met Amy Brigham recently at a Starbucks on Old Cutler Road in Miami, on a warm summer morning. We carried our coffee drinks into the Deering Estates, a county park nearby, and found a picnic table among towering royal palms. We spent the next two hours talking about foot trails and eminent domain.

Amy is an eminent domain lawyer known throughout the state for her defense of private property rights. A long corridor for any purpose has never been assembled without this authority imbedded in the Bill of Rights. We in the trails community must understand this right thoroughly. It's best we understand it from the property owner's point of view.

Amy comes from a long line of eminent domain lawyers. Her father, Toby Price Brigham, directed a large firm of eminent domain lawyers until the Florida real estate collapse in 2006. He and I were classmates at Yale. Her brother won the largest eminent domain jury verdict in Florida history in 2008. And her grandfather, E.F.P. Brigham, succeeded in his case before the Florida Supreme Court, *Dade County v. Brigham,* which determined that the state is required to cover the legal expense of any property owner who contests the award in a condemnation lawsuit. I was pleased she agreed to discuss eminent domain issues with me.

Here are a few of her comments, verbatim.

- Completing the National Scenic Trails should be a worthy goal. Trying to do so cheaply dishonors their societal worth and the constitutional principle that just compensation should be paid to landowners when their property is taken for the benefit of the public. Offering landowners less than fair compensation only creates ill will and retards the completion of trails.

- The best way to accelerate the completion of trails is to prioritize them in order of urgency, and then for legislatures to not only authorize their acquisition but also appropriate the necessary funds and set deadlines for completion, by use of eminent domain if necessary. This is how highways get built. Where there is disagreement on price, a holdout does not get to prevent completion of a highway, but does get due process of law in determining lawful compensation.

- If pedestrian trails were treated with the same dignity by policy makers, agencies and landowners alike would know there is a time within which to negotiate a voluntary sale on mutually agreeable terms, or that the price will be set by due process of law (eminent domain proceedings). How many generations of Americans will be deprived of completed trails before scenic trails are deemed as important as automotive highways?

- Trying to complete trails through "willing seller" programs is typically ineffective. In my experience, willing seller programs stagnate because of inadequate funding that promotes lowball offers by agencies, which in turn promotes a holdout mindset by landowners.

- Cynicism about "willing seller" programs is prevalent now because of how so many have been conducted like battles of attrition and have become no more than a code name for uncompensated land-banking. The typical "willing seller" scheme is to publicly earmark property for future public acquisition, possibly collaborate among agencies to have the land downzoned or otherwise protected in comprehensive plans or zoning documents, wait a long time and then to offer the landowner a price that reflects the value depreciation caused by having been so earmarked.

- In addition to delay tactics, the practice of checkerboarding is also a hallmark of "willing seller" schemes (a deliberate acquisition of scattered parcels to render access or assemblage of the remaining project footprint nearly impossible, further depreciating the land of the holdouts).

- Illegal exaction of earmarked corridors is also a related problem. When a landowner seeks to entitle or improve land through which an earmarked corridor runs, agencies often leverage the need for a permit or other land use approval to exact an easement or title to the corridor as a condition of approval. (This extortive practice has been repeatedly condemned by courts.) Ironically, owners who decline lowball offers or who fight exactions are branded "unwilling sellers" and forced to either initiate litigation or wait years until the government provides due process to determine compensation (eminent domain), if it ever does. Battles of attrition like these breed distrust and resentment, and only increase the stubbornness of holdouts. The outcome is incomplete projects or decades of delay. I know of many instances where the deep offenses of a "willing seller" program created generational holdouts.

- Techniques are available (in addition to fair appraisal and adequate funding) which could incentivize completion of trails by including density transfers, where meaningful, and enhanced tax benefits for the donation of land or easements. But the value of the corridor itself is often less an issue than the negative impact of the loss of privacy on remaining lands. Finding ways to offer reliable mitigation for this could be key to accelerating completion of scenic trails. Investing in buffering, security measures and insurance policies for adjacent landowners could be meaningful inducements to sell. Enacting regulations governing the use of trails could further allay legitimate landowner concerns inherent to opening private lands for public access (trespassing, vandalism, voyeurism, loitering, un-permitted camping, littering, etc.). Funding trail rangers to enforce the considerate use of trails may be as important to completing trails as funding the land acquisition itself—no less than funding for park rangers has been vital to our national parks beyond their acquisition. I think many have overlooked how the commitment necessary to maintaining the safety of trails is vital to acquiring them in the first place. When I have been able to negotiate adequate buffering, security and considerate use regulations, my clients have become more willing sellers of corridors through their private property.

- Thinking outside the box: Acquiring trail segments through revocable easements should be explored as a means of enlisting landowner cooperation, giving them the comfort level that, if repeated trespassing or violation of trail regulations occur within defined periods, easements can be revoked. While the idea of a revocable easement might not initially appeal to hiking associations or agencies because of the potential for the disassembling of a trail, something is better than nothing—it would be superior to a complete holdout and never trying to make it work. The idea certainly brings into focus how accountable agencies and hiking associations are willing to be in order to reach the goal of completing scenic trails. In any event, if such an easement were revoked for violation of its terms, there is still the power of eminent domain to acquire the segment if necessary. Video monitoring, citation of violators by rangers or local police and hiker peer pressure could also go a long way to ensuring that the terms of a revocable easement are met and revocation does not occur. This would truly be a public-private partnership around a culture of respect for both trails and the privacy of adjacent lands.

9

A New Proposal for Closing the Gaps

On the website of the Partnership for the National Trails System is a one-page summary of the year's accomplishments. Below "Fundamental Challenges," it reads: "Completing the trails on the ground ... closing the gaps in the scenic trails ...."

I assure you, beyond any doubt, given their philosophy and the impositions they have placed upon themselves, this is far beyond difficult; it's impossible.

Why do state Departments of Transportation, the federal Department of Transportation, every utility and most fire stations, airports and school systems have the taking authority described in the Fifth Amendment of the Bill of Rights? Because a public use is deemed more important to society than a continued private use.

Friends of the Florida Trail Board members and I interviewed Adam Putnam after he announced his run for the governorship of Florida. We had a chance to tell our story about completing the Florida Trail. At the conclusion of our brief presentation, Adam said something like, "Maybe when you get near the end, we could use eminent domain to complete the trail." No other taking authority is structured like this; they all have the taking authority from the beginning of any project. Don King, chief of the land acquisition program for the National Park Service, put it this way: "Of course, when we walked in to see a property owner, he or she knew we had eminent domain in our back pocket." And that is how it is used everywhere and every time.

What we have is a marketing problem in attempting to close the gaps in our National Scenic Trails System, and I believe we have that problem for two reasons. We are not a utility and we are not a road department. But the Bill of Rights says that the taking must be "for public use." Hiking trails are obviously for a public use. Americans are conditioned to accept a "taking" for roads and utilities, but not much else. How about for medical reasons, environmental reasons, or for health reasons as a benefit of outdoor recreation? Our nation is prosperous enough that we need to turn our attention to other "public use" reasons that are sufficiently important.

The other problem is that eminent domain has been abused. State governments have taken properties in a liberalized approach to public use. Good examples of this are found under the rubric of urban blight. City officials salivated over taking ramshackle homes adjacent to urban areas and selling a large parcel of assembled land to a corporation or urban developer while knowing that a huge development will bring enormous tax revenues. All this came to a head in the famous *Kelo v. City of New London, CT*. Fifteen homes were taken from people of modest means so Pfizer, a real estate developer, and the city of New London could all have a spanking-new project close to downtown. Susan Kelo and six other property owners fought it. They never could have sustained the legal fees for three years, but a libertarian nonprofit, Institute for Justice, stepped in to help. The suit went to the Supreme Court and the court ruled against *Kelo*. The property has been idle ever since, but the case created a firestorm of protest, the largest Supreme Court outburst in the 20th century. Since then, 44 states have passed legislation to blunt this ruling, including my state of Florida. I agree that the grasping hand of government should have been slapped down in the *Kelo* case.

If there is one long, thin corridor over 1,000 miles anywhere in America that was completed without eminent domain, then I would agree—maybe, just maybe—a trail could be completed without it. But I have found none. On the other hand, we have a prototype of our own, the 1968 National Trails System Act. Eminent domain saved the Appalachian Trail for posterity. There were 2,550 takings over 700 miles. One third of the Appalachian Trail was unprotected in the 1960s. In those 2,550 takings, eminent domain was used approximately 400 times, mostly to cure titles.

But here's the significant statistic: only 100 times was it used adversarially, where the property owner dug in in an effort to prevent the taking; that's approximately one in 25 cases. Was the disruption of the lives of those 100 people worth it? That's not an easy question to answer, but I think the answer is yes. Three million people set foot on the Appalachian Trail last year.

In 1934, when the Great Smoky Mountains National Park was created, 1,100 families, perhaps 4,000 or 5,000 people, were removed from the hollows of Tennessee and western North Carolina mountains. Last year, 11 million people enjoyed the park. Were those takings worth it? Again, not an easy question, but I think the answer is yes.

Last year, at 5:00 a.m., in the La Fonda Hotel in Santa Fe, I had an epiphany that I want to share with you. What loss is most feared when a property owner sees eminent domain coming? The overwhelming concern is the loss of his or her home. A hiking trail meanders. And hikers want to be as far away from houses as possible. Jim Snow, retired attorney for the U.S. Forest Service, responsible for 25% of the A.T. takings, said, "To my knowledge, no one was asked to leave his or her home as we acquired right-of-way."

Let's draft a bill that excludes the possibility of taking a home in acquiring trail right-of-way. Could this restriction alone break the gridlock of the negative attitude toward eminent domain? I think it can. It's reasonable. And, in fact, I readily think that we should restrict ourselves in this way. You could call this a solution in plain sight, but there it is.

I am preparing a letter today, addressed to Tim Kaine, a senator from Virginia. On his website's home page is a picture of him with a backpack on, at a prominent point on a trail. He might help us move forward with the compromise I am proposing. If not, we will find our own Goodloe Byron in due time. Goodloe was the congressman who helped more than anyone to see that the 1968 National Trails System Act was passed and that the 1978 amendment was passed as well.

I have been in real estate for 60 years, buying, selling and brokering only vacant land. Years ago a utility took a 160-foot-wide, two-mile-long swath from acreage I managed. I have two eminent domain cases pending right now. I am no stranger to the process. Believe me when I tell you, no 1,000-mile-long corridor will ever be completed without it. And most of our iconic National Scenic Trails are much longer.

There are 47.9 million hikers in America who get outside on a footpath 14 or more times a year. If just a small portion of this cohort were marshaled in Washington to serve as the squeaky wheel, a 1968 act would happen again. It's painful to read in hiking club literature and elsewhere that we are going to complete our National Scenic Trails with public and private partnerships. It's been said we couldn't even get a majority of Americans to approve the U.S. Constitution, if it came to a vote. Even a small condominium association could not alter its documents if a 100% vote were required. I once tried to change five deed restrictions on 70 acres of land and couldn't get 15 people to agree. Without eminent domain, a continuous footpath requires 100% agreement to sell by property owners in the trail alignment; otherwise, there are gaps.

Our clubs have picked the ripe fruit. Adding trail miles now, through negotiations, is coming to a standstill. Last year I saw that the Pacific Crest Trail Association spent $2.5 million on land acquisition. For that large sum they secured only 1.65 miles of new treadway; the rest went for "viewshed." The Ice Age Trail, when I was there, added 10 miles that year, with 500 miles to go. My own Florida Trail added over 30 miles two years ago, but three years before lost 47 miles.

If we reject the taking authority granted to governments in the Fifth Amendment of the Bill of Rights, then I think we should be upfront with everyone: 10 of our 11 National Scenic Trails will never be completed. They will languish, underutilized—not the great recreational asset they were meant to be. I, for one, can't accept that. Will this proposal give our National Scenic Trails what they desperately need?

10

Remaining Thoughts

The Partnership for the National Trails System publishes the "State of the Trail Report." It's full of good data that illustrates the value of trails and the costs. I have the 2019 report in hand. The 11 National Scenic Trails and 19 National Historic Trails, maintained by volunteers, total 14,128 miles. They are open to the public. Collectively, Americans invested $75.6 million in these trails that year. Volunteer hours, at the Department of Interior's hourly rate for this work, represent a contribution of $25 million added to this amount. So do dollar contributions by hikers to trail nonprofits of $14.37 million. (Federal funding totaled $28.73 million.)

These figures, however, don't reveal the full story of volunteer commitment to trails in this country. The history of the Appalachian Trail tells a more accurate one. Work began in earnest to build a footpath from Maine to Georgia in 1927. Its official opening was held in 1937. Volunteers built it. Not until 1968 did the federal government make a significant commitment to trails. Each of our national trails is assigned to either the Department of Agriculture and thus to the U.S. Forest Service, or to the Department of Interior and thus to the National Park Service. These are the links that join the private sector to the federal government. Federal funds enter trails through these departments. I maintain that if Congress cut funding for trails to a trickle, federal oversight of our national trails would also drop to a trickle, but volunteers would keep these trails open for everyone, in any event.

While we are discussing the "State of the Trail Report," we must look at some other figures. The report states that 14,128 miles of trail were maintained. Continuity is not the essential element for a Historic Trail as it is for a footpath. Roadside panels can identify the historic route of the Oregon Trail, for example. So, let's say all trails maintained in 2019 were footpaths. The report goes on to say that 188 miles of new trail were built that year. In other words, less than 1.5% of the total miles were added to our national footpaths and our Historic Trails. Take a look at my numbers: Total alignment of our 10 National Scenic Trails, the footpaths, is over 16,000 miles. Miles of gaps total 4,074 miles of that total. If the 188 miles of new trail were all footpath miles, we only added 4.6%—less than 5%.

You might say we would have a shot at closing the gaps in 20 years (4.6% rounded up to 5% equals one twentieth of the gaps, or 20 years to buy all parcels). But don't think that for a minute. The ripe fruit gets picked first. We build a trail through public land first. In Florida that's three large national forests, state forests, state parks, holdings of the water management districts, military bases and so on. The picking gets tough very quickly. A few years ago we lost more miles of the Florida Trail than we gained.

Some Florida Trail history supports this statement. The Florida Trail was added to the National Trails System in 1983. Government funds became available to buy acreage for their Florida Trail right-of-way after that date. From early trail guides of the FT, we know that in 1985 the FT was 713.3 miles long. In 1992, seven years later, the FT was 944.7 miles long, a difference of 231.4 miles.

I asked Sandra Friend, author of seven guides to the Florida Trail since 2002, if she could document trail mileage over the years. She shared the following. (Totals in the list currently include two loop trails. While that adds miles to the trail, we are concerned here with the rate of growth only.)

2003: 1,395.2
Source: *Florida Trail Companion Guide for Long Distance Hikers, First Edition*

2005: 1,411.7
Source: *Florida Trail Companion Guide for Long Distance Hikers, Second Edition*

2007: 1,413.0
Source: *Florida Trail Companion Guide for Long Distance Hikers, Third Edition*

2013: 1,430.0
Source: *The Florida Trail Guide, First Edition*

2015: 1,442.3
Source: *The Florida Trail Guide, Second Edition*

2017: 1,447.6
Source: *The Florida Trail Guide, Third Edition*

2021: 1,451.1
Source: Florida National Scenic Trail, Guthook Guides' app

To conclude, in the 1980s and '90s over a seven-year period, the Florida Trail Association extended the trail by 231.4 miles, or 33.1 miles per year. From 2003 to 2021, 18 years, the FTA extended its trail by 56 miles, or 3.1 miles per year, 1/10 of the earlier rate of growth. The obvious explanation (I can assure the reader it was not a lack of effort): As the trail was being extended through public land, it could grow quickly. Once the FTA had to begin negotiations with private property owners, the rate of growth fell dramatically. The fall in growth will continue to drop because private property owners who want to help will step forward, leaving the owners who simply don't want the trail on their property, which drives growth down further. Since some will hold out indefinitely, the trail will stop growing before it is complete.

This year of 2020 is unique. People are desperate to get outside, but also to keep their distance. Not surprisingly, a *New York Times* headline read: "As Hiking Surges During the Pandemic ..." in a report about trail accidents. As hiking surges, overcrowding becomes inevitable and dirt trails can degrade quickly.

The most sensible recreational solution for everyone is in plain sight: Complete the trails we have identified as our great trails.

In Florida, 20 million people live on or near the coasts. Our trail meanders up through the center of peninsular Florida. At its widest, Florida is only 150 miles across. Most of us can get to a stretch of trail in an hour or so. Our trail should have plenty of use. It's been open for more than 50 years. Instead, we have 365,000 visitors. The Appalachian Trail receives over 3 million. We hike in winter months when the other 10 National Scenic Trails are snowed in. Why aren't we snowed with hikers? The A.T. is continuous. Our 1,300-mile trail has 300 miles of gaps in dozens of places. *Finish the trail and they will come!*

Following are some statements from the hearing before the Subcommittee on National Parks and Recreation of the Committee on Interior and Insular Affairs, House of Representatives, 90th Congress, showing that those in government and the private sector understood eminent domain was needed.

Here is Stanley Murray, Chairman of the Appalachian Trail Conference, at the hearing on March 6 and 7, 1967: "The public benefits already received from the establishment of the Appalachian Trail are already evident. Any person may use any portion of the trail at any time

without charge, registration or other acknowledgment of use. Present users include hikers, hunters, fishermen and women, youth organizations, family groups and persons who just want to walk where the air is fresh, the woods quiet and living things grow in simple magnificence according to nature's own pattern."

Further on, Ralph Hodges, vice president of the American Forest Products Association, adds: "In regard to … condemnation, we suggest that the secretary be authorized to condemn lands only when reasonable efforts at negotiation have failed and the current prospective use of the land is such that it will impair the usefulness and attractiveness of the trail permanently."

The speakers at the hearing expressed concern for expenditures, treatment of the forest where the trail corridor was laid out, overuse and so on, but the Appalachian Trail and trails added in the future would not be incomplete or temporary. It was clear that the attitude of Congress and those who spoke on behalf of long footpaths understood that eminent domain would be part of any law. Continuity and permanence were assumed. Congress has failed to imbed these two aspects of trail creation in their legislation since 1968.

What did not emerge from the hearings and from the hard work of Don King and the team in the acquisitions section of the National Park Service—which was not then conveyed by trails leadership to the hiking community—was the importance of the details as to how the A.T. was created through eminent domain. I was part of that leadership. I should have understood and spoken up.

In July 2005, Christopher Jarvi, Associate Director of Partnerships, Interpretation and Education, Volunteers, and Outdoor Recreation, National Park Service, Department of the Interior, appeared before the House Resources Subcommittee on National Parks, concerning the National Trails System Act.

Towards the middle of his statement, we read the following:

> Only the two national scenic trails established with the Act in 1968, the Appalachian National Scenic Trail (Appalachian Trail) and the Pacific Crest National Scenic Trail (Pacific Trail) are authorized to use the Act's full set of land acquisition authorities, including the use of condemnation authority as a last resort. The next nine national scenic trails and national historic trails established between 1980 and 1983 are not permitted to use Federal funds for land acquisition *because Congress believed acquisition authority would not be needed to complete the trails* [italics added]. National trails established after 1983 are permitted to use Federal funds for land acquisition from willing sellers. These designations include specific language that protect the private property owner by clearly stating that all lands or interests in lands acquired by the Federal government to protect national trails shall be acquired by providing willing sellers the full market value through the standard Federal appraisal process. In some places, state governments have taken the lead to assemble trail corridors. Where private lands are involved, nonprofit land trusts have in some cases obtained scenic easements on those lands.

(Author's note: We know "acquisition authority" means the use of eminent domain because of the sentence that precedes it: … the A.T. and the PCT "are authorized to use the Act's full set of land acquisition authorities, including the use of condemnation authority as a last resort." "Condemnation," "eminent domain" and "the taking authority" are interchangeable in common usage.)

It has now been 53 years since the passage of the National Trails System Act and 43 years since the last oversight hearing. If the "acquisition authority" of Congress "would not be needed to complete the trails," as Jarvi asserts, we certainly would have seen evidence of this by now. There has been enormous optimism, dedication and hard work brought to the challenge of completing our trails, without enough significant results. Instead, we must say that the promise was unrealistic.

I had a private conversation with a trails leader in the U.S. Forest Service about two years ago. I asked, "Do you think (this trail) can be completed without eminent domain?" His eyes were on me as he answered "Yes." We have to save this good man with some realism. In acquiring right-of-way we have moved the needle for him with about a 2% change in five years. The simple math would require 250 years to finish the trail. But it's not that simple. As I have said, the closer you get to the end, the harder it gets. The problem is asymptotic. The trail is never completed. And that's the reality.

―――――――――――――――

It is hard for me to believe, as 2020 closes, that the uphill fight for continuity and permanence is more difficult now than it was in the 1980s, '90s and later decades. Our highways, railroads, water lines, sewer lines, internet lines and gas lines are absolutely dependent on eminent domain. I think the 90th Congress in 1968 would be aghast if they realized there are now 11 National Scenic Trails but that only the one they created is continuous and secure for posterity. All the others are riddled with gaps.

But everyone who uses trails gets a finger pointed at them too. If there is a trail with no fence across it, hikers use it and take it for granted. That's more or less the motto of 47.9 million Americans who consider themselves hikers. We are taking our trails for granted. Trails don't just happen. Trails may require legislation; there may be gifts of easements; there may be large gifts of money that enable rights-of-way to be purchased. There certainly is an abundance of planning and oversight in laying out the trail and marking the route with survey tape. Then comes the difficult task of actual construction, GPS work, mapping and blazing. There's the annual job of trail maintenance. If you're new to trails, please don't take them for granted. Join a trail club and support the club that supports the trail. Please see Appendix 2.

Here is my recommendation of what to tell Congress about our National Trails System when we get their attention. An oversight hearing is the ultimate arena to present this list:

- We want uniformity in a National Trails System, so hikers will know what to expect when they head off on a national trail. There is none today, so please set the standard. And by all means, call on the thru-hikers who have walked these long trails from beginning to end. They will gladly offer their important opinions.

- Complete our National Scenic Trails. They are woefully incomplete. A trail with gaps is like an interstate with gaps. The number of people drawn to either is a fraction of those who would enjoy a continuous footpath as they would a highway.

- Each existing National Scenic Trail should be reviewed. Not all are deserving of the title. One of them looks like it was placed in the wrong category. Perhaps another category should be created. Only Congress can do this.

- Are there trails that need to be added? I can think of one that has been waiting too long for recognition. Review of this sort is needed.

- Change some names. All trails in the National Trails System are scenic. But we call hiking trails alone National Scenic Trails. Aren't Recreation Trails and Historic Trails scenic? My recommendation: Call all trails National Scenic Trails. Call our top footpaths National Hiking Trails.

- Provide us with an exact definition of a National Hiking Trail: minimum length, minimum services we'll find, the trail club responsible, minimum and maximum grade. Again, the thru-hikers can help with this.

- Through the clubs, provide most support for the weakest clubs. Encourage the strongest to leave the nest instead of soaking up funds. Except for acquiring rights-of-way and scenic easements— which is the government's job—volunteers can do the rest.

I have made it clear that I see no possible way of completing our trails without eminent domain, and yet the climate for the use of eminent domain is intensely negative. What to do? Without it we are dead. With it we see rejection everywhere. Chances are slimmer than slim. Without it, zero; with it, close to zero.

We should go with "close to zero." Here is how continuous trails, secure for posterity, can be made to happen. With certainty. There is no doubt in my mind. I just can't provide a date.

The quicker we can involve every hiker in America, the quicker we will see results. This is not a task for the board members of hiking clubs alone. This is a task for everyone. We must create a conversation. We must talk openly about eminent domain—to hikers, to strangers, to every elected official. Don't treat it like an offensive term. It's not. Today and for years past we have been intimidated in spite of the fact that eminent domain is absolutely essential for any complex society and is used daily. We must ask questions plentifully and make bold statements cautiously, except this: Foot trails need to be continuous.

We use eminent domain for utilities and travel corridors. Why not hiking trails? Hiking trails have much the same problems in the acquisition stage. It's only the final use that's different.

Any neighborhood is enhanced by a scenic easement with an unpaved footpath meandering through it. We are an affluent society. We can afford this. Aren't health issues as important today as transportation issues? Foot trails are an inexpensive, democratic contribution to society. Provide clubs with the right-of-way; they will do the rest. No expensive infrastructure. No trained staff needed to run things. Other forms of exercise and leisure don't need corridors; we aren't opening floodgates for another dozen similar uses. Acquiring footpaths is not something the general population can provide. But provide the right-of-way in a scenic easement and hikers will do the rest. Hikers will maintain the footpath; everyone will enjoy it.

When you explain that all corridors need eminent domain, you will get objections. Be patient. Talk about it. Push for sympathetic friends with speaking ability to talk to groups. Push for friends with writing ability to write for newsletters. Talk to elected officials in your district. See if you can find some to support the cause. What we can't do is pick the timetable. What we need to do is till the soil properly until it rains and the sun comes out.

The Civil Rights Act of 1964 was a huge step forward in securing rights for African Americans. We plateaued. Abuses surfaced, but time and again it seemed that for years the black community and its supporters couldn't keep that progress moving forward.

And then one day in Minneapolis, for eight minutes a police officer kept his knee on the neck of an unarmed, handcuffed black man prostrate on the ground until he died—a wake-up call for the nation. Changes in every aspect of society are taking place. We all see it. Sadly, the truth is that even though a cause is justified, society often fails to respond. The true believers must keep the cause alive, waiting for a "George Floyd moment." Hikers must do this if they want continuous trails. If they do, their time will come.

Examples are everywhere. Here is a "George Floyd moment."

A controversy over the name "Washington Redskins" goes back at least until 1933, one year after the organization was formed. Critics of the name, in 1971, considered it a racist slur. Washington journalists provided extensive coverage of the subject and why it was offensive.

In 1972, team president Edward Bennett Williams defended the name and said it was meant to convey respect, but activists were not appeased and pressed for a name change.

During Super Bowl XXVI, in 1992, the Redskins played the Buffalo Bills in Minneapolis. Three thousand demonstrators protested the name. Native American leaders also sought to strip the team of the name.

1999: The Federal Trademark Trial and Appeal Board called the name disparaging and ruled against the owners, but they successfully appealed in federal court.

2009: A Native American individual appealed, but lost.

2013: Redskins owner Dan Snyder vowed that the team wouldn't change its name. "We'll never change the name. It's that simple ... NEVER ... you can use caps," Snyder told reporters. He stated that the name change was chosen in 1933 to honor Native Americans.

July 2020: The team announced it will retire the name. The new name, possibly temporary, is "Washington Football Club." Well, well, well. A "George Floyd moment."

If hikers in America want their 11 national hiking trails continuous and secure, their persistence will for sure pay off. It is time to get to work, beginning and ending with Congress and the National Trails System Act.

APPENDIX 1

A PERSONAL CRITICAL SUMMARY OF
11 NATIONAL SCENIC TRAILS

Appalachian Trail (A.T.)

The Appalachian Trail sprang into the mind of Benton MacKaye around 1920, as part of a bigger idea. He envisioned a series of small farms and wilderness study camps for city dwellers, running the length of the Appalachian Mountains and connected by a trail. This idea, titled *An Appalachian Trail: A Project in Regional Planning*, appeared in print in 1921. By 1937 the trail was considered complete at about 2,000 miles. There have been many reroutings over the years. The trail today is considered 2,190 miles long.

In 1961 I talked my younger brother into joining me for an overnight hike on the A.T. We made it from Clingman's Dome to Fontana Dam. I still have the permit issued us, dated July 11. Grossly unprepared for the adventure, we had a miserable time, which I painfully recount in *Trail Reflections: 50 Years of Hiking and Backpacking*. Since then I have hiked the A.T. in 11 of the 14 states through which the trail passes.

Worldwide, I don't think there is a footpath better known or more highly used. About 3 million people set foot somewhere on the A.T. during 2019. It is doubtful that use of the other 10 trails combined exceeds this number.

In 1968 Congress recognized its role in outdoor recreation when it passed the National Trails System Act. It granted eminent domain to the A.T., so 700 miles of a 2,100-mile trail could be acquired, making it continuous and secure over its entire length—from Springer Mountain in Georgia to Mount Katahdin in Maine. Since '68, Congress has added 10 more trails to the National Trails System.

The problem is that the A.T. today is so far ahead of the other 10, they'll never catch up unless Congress lends a hand. In what ways? Bigger membership by far, bigger budget by far. Much more influence in Washington. More staff. And the imbalance continues. On February 6, 2020, the Partnership for the National Trails System went to Congress for financial support for the A.T., asking for $5.45 million of $17.64 million, 30.8% of the funds provided for our National Scenic Trails—even though the A.T. is the only one with a continuous treadway. It spent the money on "viewshed." Congress needs to weigh in.

Arizona National Scenic Trail (AZT)

Of the 11 National Scenic Trails, three are entirely within one state. The Arizona Trail begins on the US-Mexico border and follows mountain ridges over 800 miles north, to the border with Utah. If you think of heat when you think of Arizona, don't be dissuaded. Pick your season for the weather you want, from 104 degrees to deep snow. The Arizona Trail Association (ATA) likes October through November and March through April. I'd pick the first week of December.

Not many trails are described as is the Arizona Trail: mesas, deserts, arroyos, sagebrush and juniper woodland, exposed snowy ridges, quiet ponderosa forests.

The association hasn't had the gap problems that haunt all other long trails except the A.T. because it lies entirely on public land. Almost entirely. There are some preferred alignments here and there on private land that someday may be AZ corridors, but "entirely on public land" is as close to accurate here as anywhere except the A.T.

I have connected with the AZ on the Bright Angel Trail in Grand Canyon National Park, south of Flagstaff and east of Patagonia, just a few miles north of the Mexican border. I love the dry air, the ponderosa pine at elevation and the cold, starry nights.

There is one issue the AZ's membership will be wrestling with for years to come: water. As you plan a hike, be sure you know where your water will come from, at least once every day at a minimum.

In the late summer of 2019, the ATA installed a 1,500-gallon rainwater collector, of their own design, in a particularly remote segment—halfway between the Gila River and a windmill near Picketpost Trailhead. This 21-mile segment has been the site of many search-and-rescue operations. Water quality will be studied for a year. If the experiment proves successful, more collectors will undoubtably be built.

For updates on water availability go to the ATA's "Water Report Online." They also recommend Guthook Guides' smartphone app. I would have a personal locator device if traveling alone, as well.

Continental Divide Trail National Scenic Trail (CDT)

A hiking friend of mine was visiting Yellowstone National Park with his wife and sought out a ranger to ask an innocuous question. Did the ranger know where the Continental Divide Trail came through Yellowstone? The ranger admitted he didn't know what the CDT was. Larry tried not to show his consternation and annoyance. It's one of the 11 National Scenic Trails, one of the Big Three, along with the Appalachian Trail and the Pacific Crest Trail. Second only to the North Country Trail in length, the CDT stretches from the Mexican border to the Canadian border. It came through the park. They probably weren't far from it at that moment. But the ranger was no help.

The Continental Divide Trail begins on the Mexican border, 90 miles south of Hachita, New Mexico, population 60. Nothing was there but a picnic table when I visited in 2010.

A one-time experience does not a statistic make, but while I stopped to read a panel where the trail crosses State Road 9 in southern New Mexico, a jeep pulled over and two large people piled out of the back. They spoke with an accent. They had flown from Germany to El Paso the day before and decided to get in shape to hike the CDT by hiking from El Paso to the point on State Road 9 where the CDT crosses the trail. I joined them for a couple of hours. The next day I ran into a threesome, one from Seattle, one from Portland and the third from Germany, also doing the entire CDT. Two days later I met three Israelis and a Parisian who had joined them. These nine hikers, seven from other countries, were the only people I saw on the trail during my first three days.

This 3,100-mile trail ends at Waterton Lakes, Canada. There is no customs agent there, so it's best to head for Chief Mountain Customs Station on Montana Highway 17. The northerly 800 miles of the trail passes through some of our most spectacular scenery, including in Glacier National Park, the Bob Marshall Wilderness Area and the Anaconda-Pintler Wilderness.

Sadly, there are 800 miles of backcountry roads, 510 miles of which permit motorized vehicles. Hopefully that will change over time. The Continental Divide Trail has strong leadership. They get things done.

Florida National Scenic Trail (FT)

My scrapbook holds a copy of a permit dated July 11, 1961, which I needed for my younger brother and me to hike on the Appalachian Trail from Clingman's Dome to Fontana Dam in Smoky Mountains National Park. I was 27. Rich was 17. We took blankets off our motel beds, rolled some canned food inside, slung them over our shoulders in bandoleer fashion and were ready for our hike. Our parents drove us to Clingman's Dome and off we went, our first ever backpacking trip.

I open *Trails Reflections: 50 Years of Hiking and Backpacking* with "A Miserable First Trip," the story of that hike. I won't recount it again here, but the title tells you something! The odd result of that hike surfaced on the drive home. Was there a long-distance hiking trail in Florida, I wondered. I couldn't find any evidence of one. So why not build one? It was that simple.

Hike in Florida? Heat, thunderstorms, mosquitos, no-see-ums, deer flies, ticks. What's to like about the idea?

Rotate the calendar six months and everything changes. Insects mostly vanish. Frost, many nights. Surprisingly diverse habitats: palm hammocks, prairies, longleaf pine islands, springs, vistas across marshland at many points, panthers you'll never see—and no grizzlies. At first you might miss the long climbs and steep descents, but you'll get over it.

The volunteers built and now maintain 1,584 miles of the Florida Trail, which includes a loop in Central Florida plus side trails. The thru-hiker will do 1,130 miles from Oasis Visitor Center on Highway 41, the Tamiami Trail in South Florida, to Gulf Islands National Seashore near Pensacola.

Like all National Scenic Trails except the Appalachian Trail, there are gaps in this trail consisting of 300 miles of private property, requiring road walks for the end-to-end hiker on the Florida Trail. These miles aren't just in one place or in a dozen places. They are scattered up and down the trail.

The weather is excellent for four months, December through March. That's longer than our high-use, long trails. In North Florida, April weather is also often pleasant enough. There is only one National Scenic Trail free of snow in these months.

Ice Age National Scenic Trail (IAT)
and
North Country National Scenic Trail (NCT)

Along the Ice Age Trail, stretches of the footpath are called "segments"; along the Arizona Trail, such stretches are called "passages" and along the Florida Trail, "sections." Curious that these three trails have chosen different words, the only trails entirely within one state. The word in common parlance used for the remaining eight of the 11 NSTs is "section."

I saw Mike Wollmer, executive director of the Ice Age Trail Alliance, at several Outdoor Retailer shows and had some helpful correspondence with Bruce Matthews, retiring executive director of the North Country Trail Association, and was aware that their offices were not that far from each other. So for several years I considered the obvious: visit Cross Plains (near Madison, Wisconsin), meet Mike Wollmer and set foot on the Ice Age Trail, and then visit Lowell (near Grand Rapids, Michigan), meet Bruce Matthews and set foot on the North Country Trail. Both were willing to see me, so I got to hike in states I had visited only once—technically, at that.

Mike arranged for me to see the IAT with Kevin Thusius, head of land acquisition. Kevin knew the trail well; he also knew his birds. I have been a birder since age 11. A treat for me. The photographs of the trail posted on the website give a very good introduction to what the hiker finds.

When I saw the Ice Age Trail, back in 2017, Kevin Thusius told me their proposed trail was 1,200 miles long and that 653 miles were open to the public. They were acquiring 10 to 15 miles a year. At 10, that's over 50 years to go; at 15, that's over 35 years to go. What has not been considered is that as a project like this nears completion, land acquisition becomes ever more difficult. Today they are acquiring closer to one mile per year.

Back in Lowell, Bruce Matthews had arranged a lunch with the entire staff. We ate outside in pleasant weather, where I got a chance to meet Andrea Ketchmark, the incoming executive director. From Lowell I drove north on Highway 37, enjoyed a leisurely lunch on the water in Traverse City and then crossed the Mackinac Bridge to the Upper Peninsula. I made a beeline for Munising and the next day was hiking on the North Country Trail, toward Munising Falls. I also explored Grand Island, Michigan, before heading back to Madison, Wisconsin. There are delightful stretches that trail hikers should see.

The trail's full name is the North Country National Scenic Trail. It is the longest by far of our 11 National Scenic Trails. The Continental Divide National Scenic Trail is the second longest, but very much shorter, at 3,100 miles. The North Country Trail lives up to the term "north country." It is never very far from our border with Canada as it passes through North Dakota, Minnesota, Wisconsin, Michigan, Ohio, Pennsylvania, New York and Vermont. (See frontis map.) It crosses hundreds of thousands of acres of national and state forests, valleys, farmland, prairies, lakes and streams, including the Great Lakes and the famed Adirondack Mountains. Miles available to hikers: 2,814.

I am overwhelmed, however, by the gaps in the North Country Trail. A recent update shows 1,988 miles of gaps in a 4,702-mile trail. Bruce Matthews thinks eminent domain is a nonstarter as a way to acquire a hiking trail right-of-way. But "negotiations," "public and private partnerships," and "collaborative efforts" as a way of completing a trail won't get us there. (See my last chapter and the uncontestable data in chapters 5, 7 and 8.)

Natchez Trace National Scenic Trail (NTT)

The Natchez Trace National Scenic Trail has puzzled me for years.

I neither hear nor read accounts of hikes there and find no appealing description of the treadway or the views. The web page, "A walk through History," from the National Parks Service, provides an inviting photograph of the treadway, but I am at once confused by the text. The title stresses history, so I wonder if this trail is misplaced. Is it a historical trail misidentified as a hiking trail? The site goes on, "The 450-mile foot trail that became known as the Natchez Trace was the lifeline through the Old Southwest." That was then, when America ended at the Mississippi River. The Trace extended from Nashville, TN across the extreme northwest corner of Alabama to Natchez, MS…"today there are five separate trails totaling over 60 miles…" Unfortunately only 60 miles of hiking trail have been built in five discontinuous sections since 1983.

I didn't have to walk far before I saw evidence of earlier trail improvements that were now tawdry. Boards had been laid down, for example, to make sodden soil walkable, but the boards were now in serious decay. But I had a bigger complaint: the traffic noise. I don't think I was ever out of earshot of cars on the parkway while I hiked.

If we study the first five trails chosen to be national scenic trails, we quickly see that this trail does not qualify. The average length of those first five is over 2,500 miles. This was a trail idea hatched in Washington, D.C., not one needed by hikers living in the area of the trace, Nashville to Natchez. Senator Phil Burton from

California saw to it that the Natchez Trace Trail became a National Scenic Trail. Burton probably hoped that a hiking path would be built and used to match the 444 miles of parkway. That never happened. What did happen was on the very same date Congress lowered the definition of a minimum length for a National Scenic Trail to 100 miles. Almost 40 years later the Natchez Trace Trail has still not qualified for that minimum length. We need to clean this up. One more reason for an oversight hearing. Perhaps the Natchez Trace Trail can qualify as a Historic Trail.

New England National Scenic Trail (NET)

My impression of the New England Trail: A lot of hikers must care about this trail, particularly members of the Appalachian Mountain Club and the Connecticut Forest and Park Association.

It was not easy for me to find the trail west of Holyoke in Massachusetts. When I finally found Route 202 west of town, I found a 12" x 24" sign that read: NEW ENGLAND TRAIL, and I was on my way.

In Connecticut I was joined by Hiking Trails for America board member Larry Luxenberg. We took I-691 west to Hwy. 71, eventually finding Park Drive, and took it to the Merimere Reservoir. A delightful climb along the edge of a vertical rock face, with spectacular views into the reservoir, brought us to Castle Rock, a high point in the area, and more grand vistas. Larry and I ended the day in Guilford, enjoying a pasta dish (Larry) and a crabmeat salad (Jim). The following day I returned to Guilford Harbor to relax in an Adirondack chair near the water, site of the southern terminus where I had first set foot on the NET two days earlier. If you want to start your hike in Guilford, drive south of town on Route 77, to the Guilford Harbor. Ask anyone where the bocci court is. Nearby, you will find a kiosk identifying the southern terminus of the trail.

Often, the trail, where it crosses roads, is hard to find. But I found the trail itself well blazed, wide from use and full of rocks from all those glaciers way back when.

Pacific Crest National Scenic Trail (PCT)

There is a special place in my memory for the Pacific Crest Trail. Not long after founding the Florida Trail Association to build and maintain the Florida Trail in the spring of 1966, I thought we ought to schedule some adventures outside Florida for our members. These activities might be welcome, particularly in the summer when it was too hot to hike our trail. It was the fall of 1968 when I got the idea of scheduling a hike on the John Muir Trail. Eight of us met in Fresno. We hiked out of Kings Canyon to the John Muir Trail, south on this trail to a point where we could descend into Sequoia National Park. I remember we did 6,000 feet up that first day, with frost on our sleeping bags in a meadow the following morning. We were young. And you had to search for written rules back then. For Florida hikers this was another world: the dry air, the smell of ponderosa pine, powder-like dirt in the treadway, a pine grosbeak, bristlecone pines at altitudes above 10,000 feet. "Climb the mountains and get their good tidings. ..." What country John Muir enjoyed!

You can shoulder your pack in Campo on the Mexican border and hike the 2,650 miles to the Canadian border on the PCT and not know that, unlike the A.T., about 10% of this trail is not secure because the treadway is open for you. The Pacific Crest Trail Association (PCTA) is actively trying to negotiate their last miles because they are reluctant to use eminent domain.

To understand how difficult that is, in a recent year the PCTA members gave 104,269 hours to the trail, an in-kind value of $2.4 million. They gave another $2.5 million in private funds to supplement $964,000 in government grants and acquired much valuable viewshed, but acquired only 1.56 miles of treadway!

The treadway is not everything, but it's almost everything. If the hiker had a safe, secure treadway through the treatment ponds of a sewer system in order to enjoy the next 100 miles of the PCT, it would be worth it.

I'm afraid the PCTA is buying viewshed because they don't want to use eminent domain to buy what they really must have. Eminent domain was used to complete the A.T. in 1/6 of the parcels acquired over 700 miles. It was absolutely essential for one parcel in 25, about 100 properties, because they were adversarial takings. The owners tried not to sell. How does the PCTA intend to escape this statistic—easily a large enough sample to describe the challenge ahead of them?

I've been back to this glorious trail since the hike described above. In fact, in 2010 I day-hiked the PCT in 12 separate places, from the Cascades to I-10. It can't be beat.

Pacific Northwest National Scenic Trail (PNTS)

When one looks at a U.S. map, the Pacific Northwest Trail makes a lot of sense. Start it in the mountains of the Continental Divide. And, by the way, we have one of our most spectacular national parks right there, servicing as a trailhead: Glacier National Park. The trail then winds west through Whitefish Divide, the Purcells, Selkirks, Kettles, Cascades and Olympic National Parks to the Pacific Ocean at Cape Alava, WA.

This route was conceived by Ron Strickland in 1970. Strickland and others did much fieldwork on the trail for the next six years. In 1977 he founded the Pacific Northwest Trail Association after several thru-hikes of the proposed route; two of the thru-hikers appeared on the cover of *Backpacker* magazine, introducing the PNTS to readers.

In 1977 Congress authorized a study to determine if the PNTS was worthy of National Scenic Trail designation. The conclusion of the report was a no.

Like a true entrepreneur, Strickland didn't take that lying down. In 1983 he hiked the entire length of the PNTS with Ted Hitzroth, the cartographer for the Pacific Northwest Trail Association, which Strickland and others had created six years earlier.

Through the 1980s and '90s the trail and the association saw steady growth. In the early 2000s, sections of the trail received National Recreational Trail designation, including one in Glacier National Park.

In 2000 Congressman Norm Dicks and Senator Maria Cantwell introduced the Pacific Northwest Scenic Trail designation to Congress. Congress passed the Omnibus Public Lands Management Act of 2009 on March 25, and President Barack Obama signed it on March 30.

The act placed the management of the PNTS with the U.S. Forest Service, an agency of the U.S. Department of Agriculture. A management plan was to be produced within two years. As of this writing, it has not yet been produced.

Of the 1,200 miles of alignment of the PNTS, 900 miles of trail have been built and 300 miles are in gaps.

Potomac Heritage National Scenic Trail (PHT)

Unlike the A.T., PCT and the CDT, the Potomac Heritage National Scenic Trail is not just one thing. South of Washington, DC, it is primarily a bike trail. By the time this trail reaches Point Lookout in Chesapeake Bay, even the bike lane beside Route 5 has disappeared and the cyclist must bike in the car lane.

Back in DC, the path—on the west side of the Potomac River and opposite the Lincoln Memorial and the Washington Monument—lies within the expanded, wooded right-of-way for the George Washington Parkway. The river is usually a stone's throw away; so is the parkway, with the path between them. While the lush foliage is easy on the eyes, the traffic noise assails the ears.

In the vicinity of the G. W. Parkway, the path is paved, at least five feet wide and very popular. On a Wednesday about noon there were only a few parking spaces left. Cyclists with professional-looking headgear competed for paved space with joggers, walkers and baby carriages. In spite of the crowd, I saw no accidents.

North of Harpers Ferry, I walked from the pleasant tree-lined town, across the Potomac on the A.T. foot bridge adjacent to the CSX bridge, into Maryland, and back. The hiker can walk from DC, north on the bank of the old Chesapeake and Ohio Canal all the way to Cumberland, Maryland. North of there one can walk from the C & O Canal bank to Pittsburgh on the Allegheny Passage.[14]

In their Potomac Heritage brochure, the National Park Service says we can "hike, bike, ride horseback, row or paddle the Potomac Heritage network of trails." And therein lies confusion. There is a bold line from Pittsburgh to Point Lookout on Chesapeake Bay in the brochure. The color of the line changes from forest green to purple through at least seven color changes … without a key or any explanation as to the exact meaning of each color. In three places on the map the trail is purposely discontinuous, giving the hiker the impression that the National Park Service intends to keep it that way.

Since it's called "Potomac Heritage," why does a bold green line go all the way to Pittsburgh? The route runs out of historical steam northwest of Cumberland and also runs out of the Potomac River basin. For hikers, the only impressive footpath in the system lies in this stretch, a 70-mile hike called the Laurel Highlands Hiking Trail, with campsites along the route. I wondered if planners grasped at this out-of-area trail to give legitimacy to identifying the entire mishmash as a National Scenic Trail.

The poor person who wrote the text was apparently as confused as I was. He or she called the PHT an "expanding network." That's putting it kindly. The National Park Service brochure, in fact, doesn't know how to title the brochure, so it's called simply, Potomac Heritage. It's not a trail. It is a collection of trail projects in the DC area. Given this area, these assorted trails are close to historical places, but the trails themselves aren't historical as are the Pony Express Trail and the Mormon Trail. Something should be done; I don't know what.

APPENDIX 2

HIKING CLUBS AND TRAIL-RELATED ORGANIZATIONS ACROSS AMERICA

ALASKA (AK)
- Alaska Mountain & Wilderness Huts Assoc.,
  www.alaskahuts.org

ALABAMA (AL)
- Pinhotie Trail Alliance,
  www.pinhotitrailalliance.org

ARKANSAS (AR)
- TAKAHIK River Valley Hikers,
  www.takahik.com

ARIZONA (AZ)
- Arizona Trail Association,
  www.aztrail.org
- Huachuca Hiking Club,
  groups,io/g/HuachucaHikingClub
- SaddleBrooke Hiking Club,
  www.saddlebrookehikingclub.com
- Southern Arizona Hiking Club,
  www.sahcinfo.org

CALIFORNIA (CA)
- Chico Hiking Association,
  www.chicohiking.org
- El Dorado Trail,
  www.eldoradotrail.com
- OC [Orange County] Hiking Club,
  www.oc-hiking.com
- Orinda Hiking Club, CA,
  www.orindahiking.org
- Pacific Crest Trail Association,
  www.pcta.org

COLORADO (CO)

- Colorado Fourteeners Initiative, www.14ers.org
- Colorado Mountain Club, www.cmcboulder.org
- Colorado Trail Foundation, www.coloradotrail.org
- Continental Divide Trail Alliance, www.cdtrail.org
- Old Spanish Trail Association, CO, www.oldspanishtrail.org
- Sand Creek Greenway, www.sandcreekgreenway.org
- Volunteers of Outdoor Colorado, www.voc.org

DISTRICT OF COLUMBIA (DC)

- American Discovery Trail Society, www.discoverytrail.org

FLORIDA (FL)

- Florida Trail Association, www.floridatrail.org

GEORGIA (GA)

- Benton MacKaye Trail Association, www.bmta.org
- Georgia Appalachian Trail Club, www.georgia-atclub.org
- Kennesaw Mountain Trail Club, www.kennesawmountaintrailclub.org

IDAHO (ID)
- Idaho Trails Association,
  www.idahotrailsassociation.org

ILLINOIS (IL)
- River to River Trail Society, Harrisburg,
  www.rivertorivertrail.com

INDIANA (IN)
- Hoosier Hikers,
  www.hoosierhikerscouncil.org

KANSAS (KS)
- Trail Masons Assoc., Shawnee,
  www.trailmasons.blogspot.com

KENTUCKY (KY)
- Pine Mountain Trail Conference,
  www.pinemountaintrail.com

LOUISIANA (LA)
- Louisiana Hiking Club,
  www.hikelouisiana.org

MASSACHUSETTS (MA)
- Appalachian Mountain Club,
  www.outdoors.org
- Essex County Trail Association,
  www.ectaonline.org

MARYLAND (MD)
- Mosaic Outdoor Mountain Club of MD,
  www.mosaicmd.org

MAINE (ME)

- Appalachian Mountain Club
  www.amcmaine.org
- Maine Appalachian Trail Club
  www.matc.org
- The Maine chapter of Women Who Hike
  www.facebook.com/groups/332781623858383/

MICHIGAN (MI)

- Hiawatha Shore to Shore,
  www.northcountrytrail.org/hss
- North Country Trail Association,
  www.northcountrytrail.org
- Polly Ann Trailway,
  www.pollyanntrailway.org

MINNESOTA (MN)

- Border Route Trail Association,
  www.borderroutetrail.org
- Boundary Waters Advisory Committee,
  www.boundarywaterstrail.org
- Superior Hiking Trail Association,
  www.shta.org

MISSOURI (MO)

- Missouri Trail Huggers,
  www.vfom.org

MONTANA (MT)

- Beartooth Recreational Trails Assoc.,
  www.beartoothtrails.org

NORTH CAROLINA (NC)

- Carolina Mountain Club,
  www.carolinamtnclub.org

- East Coast Greenway,
  www.greenway.org/nc.php

- Friends of the Mountains-to-Sea Trail,
  www.ncmst.org

- Nantahala Hiking Club,
  www.nantahalahikingclub.org

- Piedmont Hiking & Outing Club,
  www.piedmonthikingandoutingclub.org

- The Haw River Trail,
  www.thehaw.org

NORTH DAKOTA (ND)

- Buckeye Trail Association,
  www.buckeyetrail.org

- Cuyahoga Valley Trails Council,
  www.cvtrailscouncil.org

- Maah Daah Hey Trail Association,
  www.mdhta.com

NEW HAMPSHIRE (NH)

- Chatham Trails Association,
  www.chathamtrails.org

- Cohos Trail Association,
  www.cohostrail.org

- Randolph Mountain Club,
  www.randolphmountainclub.org

NEW JERSEY (NJ)
- New York-New Jersey Trail Conference, www.nynjtc.org
- Union County Hiking Club, www.uchc.org

NEW MEXICO (NM)
- New Mexico Rails-to-Trails Assoc., www.nmrailstotrails.org

NEVADA (NV)
- Carson Valley Trails Association, www.carsonvalleytrails.org
- Tahoe Rim Trail Association, www.tahoerimtrail.org

NEW YORK (NY)
- Adirondack Forty-Sixers, www.adk46er.org
- Adirondack Mountain Club, www.adk.org
- Buffalo Hiking Club, Facebook Group
- Catskill 3500 Club, www.catskill-3500-club.org
- Cayuga Trails Club, www.cayugatrailsclub.org
- Champlain Area Trails, www.champlainareatrails.com
- CNY Hiking, www.cnyhiking.com
- Crescent Trail Hiking Assoc., www.crescenttrail.org

- Finger Lakes Trail Conference, www.fingerlakestrail.org

- Foothills Trail Club, www.foothillstrailclub.org

- Long Island Greenbelt Trail Conference, www.ligreenbelt.org

- Victor Hiking Trails, www.victorhikingtrails.org

OREGON (OR)

- Corvallis to the Sea Trail, www.c2ctrail.org

- National Coast Trail Association, www.coasttrails.org

- Siskiyou Upland Trails Association, www.sutaoregon.org

- Trailkeepers of Oregon, www.trailkeepersoforegon.org

PENNSYLVANIA (PA)

- Blue Mountain Eagle Climbing Club, www.bmecc.org

- Cumberland Valley Appalachian Trail Club, www.cvatclub.org

- Keystone Trails Association, www.kta-hike.org

- Standing Stone Trail Club, www.standingstonetrail.org

- Susquehanna Appalachian Trail Club, www.satc-hike.org

TENNESSEE (TN)
- Chattanooga Hiking Club,
  www.chatthiking.com
- Cherokee Hiking Club,
  www.cherokeehikingclub.org
- Cumberland Trail Conference,
  www.cumberlandtrail.org
- The Smoky Mountains Hiking Club,
  www.smhclub.org

TEXAS (TX)
- Lone Star Hiking Trail Club,
  www.lonestartrail.org
- West Texas Trail Walkers,
  www.westtexastrailwalkers.org

UTAH (UT)
- Trails Foundation Northern Utah,
  www.tfnu.org
- Weber Pathways,
  www.weberpathways.org

VIRGINIA (VA)
- Great Falls Trail Blazers,
  www.GreatFallsTrailBlazers.org
- Natural Bridge Appalachian Trail Club,
  www.nbatc.org
- Potomac Appalachian Trail Club,
  www.patc.net
- Potomac Heritage Trail Association,
  www.potomactrail.org

- Rivanna Trails Foundation,
  www.rivannatrails.org
- Tidewater Appalachian Trail Club,
  www.tidewateratc.com

VERMONT (VT)
- Cross Rivendell Trail Association,
  www.rivendelltrail.squarespace.com
- Cross Vermont Trail Association,
  www.crossvermont.org
- Green Mountain Club,
  www.greenmountainclub.org

WASHINGTON (WA)
- Ferry County Rail Trail,
  www.ferrycountyrailtrail.com
- Pacific Northwest Trail Association,
  www.pnt.org
- Volunteers for Outdoor Washington,
  www.trail-stewards.org
- Washington Trails Association,
  www.wta.org

WISCONSIN (WI)
- Ice Age Trail Alliance,
  www.iceagetrail.org

WEST VIRGINIA (WV)
- Appalachian Trail Conservancy,
  www.appalachiantrail.org
- West Virginia Scenic Trails Assoc.,
  www.wvscenictrails.org

APPENDIX 3

MY HIKING LIFE AND EMINENT DOMAIN

Starting hiking clubs and struggling to make hiking trails continuous and secure has formed a major portion of my life. Here's a brief summary.

In July 1961 I got a permit for my brother and me to hike from Clingman's Dome in Smoky Mountain National Park to Fontana Dam. A nightmare awaited two foolish, unprepared young men. We inched into this disaster by degrees.

My dad had a great idea in the winter of 1960–61: a first-ever family vacation in the mountains of western North Carolina. Headquarters for the Kern band of seven (parents, younger brother Rich, sister Ellie and husband, my new wife Lynn and me) was a rustic motel with a pool, near Great Smoky Mountains National Park. Lynn and I would drive north from Miami; the rest would drive south from New Jersey. After two days of doing some typical touristy things, I got bored. So I proposed a hike along the Appalachian Trail to my brother. Our parents and my wife had no objection.

By using the first joint of my thumb on a hand-out map provided by the National Park Service, I concluded that the distance from our starting point at Clingman's Dome to Fontana Dam was 40 miles and that we could do it in a little over a day. I was 27 and my brother was 17. With that age difference, you know who was making the decisions. Neither of us had ever backpacked in our lives, nor did we have any of the proper equipment for an overnight hike.

We did buy a can of Sterno and canned food, took two blankets off our motel beds, rolled the canned food in the blankets, tied off each end with string and slung our "packs" over our shoulders. Brother Rich wore his tennis shoes; I had a pair of cowboy boots without laces. We were ready. So Dad drove us to the national park's Clingman's Dome. The family came and cheered as we set off after lunch.

It was a pleasant afternoon with a light breeze and bright sun. Our departure point at 6,000 feet was the highest elevation in the park, so the first couple miles were all downhill. Soon, however, the trail changed to as many ups and downs as a roller coaster. Then something else happened. Clouds started drifting through the trees, condensed on leaves and fell on us as rain. The knee-high grasses and wildflowers along the path drenched our feet.

By late afternoon we came to the first lean-to marked on the map, but realized we couldn't stay there because if we did, we wouldn't reach Fontana Dam by sunset the next day, when our parents planned to pick us up. Nor could we go on because we wouldn't get to the next shelter before dark. We had failed to bring a flashlight.

We got out our Sterno and heated a can of Dinty Moore stew and thought about our predicament. I told Rich that our only choice was to walk on until the absolute last moment of light and then sleep on the wet ground. Just as we finished the last of the stew, a black bear ambled into sight. He didn't appear eager to leave, probably sniffing the remains of our meal. So I hollered and growled and eventually he left. Bears or no bears, I still felt that we had to keep going.

The misty drizzle persisted. The leaves kept dripping. Dusk began to fall on us. We hiked on, looking for a dry place to lay our heads, but there was none. If we kept walking until it was pitch black, we wouldn't be able to see the trail—or anything else. We had to stop before that moment.

With only minutes to spare, I noticed a large fallen tree, broken off at about six feet high, with its huge trunk lying on the ground. Just above the break, the trunk forked. The upright trunk was badly decomposed, but three-foot-long slabs of bark with cambium attached could be pulled off the trunk. These we laid across the fallen trunk at the fork to make perhaps three feet of protection for our upper bodies. It was hard getting in under the slabs because the space was only about two feet high. And drizzle continued to fall on our legs. Not surprisingly, we hardly slept. It was a horrendous night.

Finally, a weak light filled the gloomy woods. We got up, stiff and cold, shook the wood debris out of our hair and off our clothes and rolled up our blankets. The wool blankets had kept us from freezing. We set off with wet legs, wet pants, wet feet and wet shoes. By late morning we came to the second lean-to and stopped for a rest and a snack.

My boots couldn't have been a worse choice for hiking in the rain. Going up hills, the balls of my feet slid back. Going down, my toes pushed into the front of the boots. There were no laces to tighten, to hold my ankles near the back of the boot. We walked for long stretches without saying much, just wishing we were someplace else.

By mid-afternoon the clouds were lifting and the rain was ending. The heat generated by our bodies was slowly drying our clothes. I had one precious item buried in my blanket roll that I was saving for the time the rain stopped … a dry pair of socks. At a quick rest break I removed my sopping pair and pulled on this clean, dry pair of athletic socks. Big mistake. My soft, wet skin had been plastered flat against those wet socks. But the dry ones dried out the soles of my feet, which then started slipping around in the socks. Now the dry wool of the socks slowly rubbed off a layer or two of skin. At the time, I didn't notice it.

Again, darkness fell across the Smokies, coming first to the deep hardwood forest. We were close to panic as we considered options, when we noticed that the trail was plunging downhill. We were slipping and sliding on the muddy ground, grabbing at trees to break our downward momentum. Could it be that this tortuous descent was the last stretch to Fontana Dam? Like the previous night, just a minute or two before total darkness we stumbled out onto pavement. There to our left was the dam, but no parents or car were in sight. On the dam a light shone from the watchman's office. We staggered over and walked in. We found the watchman reading at his desk. We told him who we were and asked if anyone had been looking for us. "Oh, yes," he said. "They waited quite some time and then left."

Any strength and hope we had evaporated. After a few totally demoralizing moments, the night watchman added that the people had left one of their two cars for us and he handed me the keys. As we drove to the motel, the headlights cut a path through complete darkness.

The next morning when I tried to get out of bed, I couldn't. I tried again. Finally I was able to stand up, but my leg muscles were so stiff, I couldn't move. And when I tried to move, the soles of my feet were so sore that I couldn't walk. Slowly, with six-inch steps I shuffled painfully to the bathroom.

Back at school, Rich was asked to write about his and his brother's first hike. He ended his report with "At no time was I happy to be there."

That expression became a family mantra. When describing some awful situation or when having a truly miserable time somewhere, a family member will likely end by saying, "At no time was I happy to be there." Rich and I know what that means.

On the long drive home to Miami after that first hike, I wondered if there were any hiking trails in Florida. I couldn't think of one. Florida is a flat state. But so what? Ups and downs can be a drag. The views can be a lot better in the Big Cypress or on the banks of the Suwannee than inside the dense forest of the Smokies. Yes, it's hot in summer, but Florida is the only state with ideal hiking weather in winter. My mind was racing. Wouldn't it be great to have a marked trail through the center of the state that cut through the wilds of Ocala National Forest and Osceola National Forest, then through Apalachicola National Forest and out into the panhandle? Why couldn't the trail be divided into sections to make it easier for volunteer groups to maintain? And why not form a Florida Trail Association (FTA) to promote the trail and provide a focus and a community for trail fans. As it turned out, all these ideas came to pass!

It's hard to believe that the idea to create a hiking trail the length of Florida came to me after the first … and worst … hike of my life, as described above.

Our Appalachian Trail hike was born on a whim. I came up with it one day and was on the A.T. the next. I had never heard of its founder, Benton MacKaye, nor did I know the names of founders of other trails, nor did I know, in fact, of any other trails. But I just asked myself a simple question: Was there a long-distance trail like this in Florida?

When I returned home, I looked into the question. No, there was none. So I formed the Florida Trail Association to promote the idea. (I got sidetracked for several years by wanting to first start a Florida geographical magazine to be called the *Florida Trail*. But then I got back on the "trail.")

So what if there were no mountains! Not everyone enjoys panting uphill and sliding down. Wet feet and mosquitoes may be more of a problem, but most hikers would use this trail in the winter months of December to March, no shorter a season than the ridge trails in the Rockies and Sierras. Also, a Florida dry season usually begins in early November, making most marshy places walkable by the first of the year. Since the entire state has sandy soil, the walking is even easy when the ground is wet. So winter hiking conditions in Florida are ideal.

To dramatize the idea of building a winter trail through Florida, I made a 160-mile, 12-day hike through typical Florida backcountry in 1966. The hike got major coverage in the media. A series of features in *The Miami Herald* concluded with a color cover article in its Sunday issue. Interested people were invited to join the newly launched Florida Trail Association. In just a few days we were 70 members strong! Now I found myself with an organization to run. Dues were a dollar a year. I picked Highlands Hammock State Park, near Sebring, as the location for our first annual meeting.

I envisioned the trail winding its way north from Big Cypress National Preserve, through the center of the state in the most remote habitats I could find, avoiding the east and west coasts of the peninsula where people live. Such a route would enable us to include Ocala National Forest, Osceola National Forest and Apalachicola National Forest. The trail would follow the banks of the Suwannee River for miles. I envisioned the trail ending somewhere in the panhandle.

I had a friend in those days who owned a single-engine plane. We both lived in Miami. He had an appointment in Tallahassee, so I outlined my plan for a hiking trail and asked if he could fly my proposed route to the capital. I arrived for the flight with an enormous roll of USGS maps, six miles to each sheet. At 120 mph, we covered the distance on one sheet in three minutes. I would quickly peel off the top sheet to get to the next one, just dumping it in the seats behind us. By the time we were halfway up the peninsula, the entire cabin of the plane was filled with uncoiled maps. They threatened to engulf the pilot and block his vision. But that scouting project laid the groundwork for the trail corridor, which has remained remarkably intact ever since.

Yet the full story of building the Florida Trail is less about "me" and more about "us." Once the basic corridor was aligned, I had to find individuals to route, mark and build trail sections, each about 25 miles long. I also thought Boy Scout troops could be enlisted to maintain these sections—an idea I couldn't get rolling—and I was ludicrously short on how long I thought the trail would be. The first brochure we published made the claim that it would be 500 miles. Today we know it is closer to 1,100 miles.

By the end of the 1960s I was spending lots of time dreaming of a continuous Florida trail—with no political friends and no idea how to make our trail complete. In 1971 someone asked me if I knew Dick Pettigrew. I said no. He said Dick is Speaker of the Florida House and lives in Miami. I said, "Do you know him?" He answered yes. My next question was, "Could you introduce me?"

In no time a meeting was scheduled. I explained the trail and the need for a continuous treadway. Dick had a Florida Trail bill drafted and filed, and not long after, a hearing was scheduled. I was about to be politically baptized by total immersion.

I went alone to the hearing. Older men filed in and took their seats. What interest might they have in this bill? In fact, I wondered why anyone would have an interest in the footpath, particularly a negative one. And then I found out.

A lobbyist for the Florida Cattlemen's Association told the assembled subcommittee that bulls would gore the hikers. Too much liability. The lobbyist from the Citrus Commission said hikers would eat the fruit off the trees. The lobbyist for the timber industry said the hikers would burn the forest down with improper campfires.

In the 1970s Florida agriculture was our biggest industry, and the Big Three had just spoken. It didn't matter what I might have to say. I was finished before I got started. I felt like a lamb led to slaughter.

For 30 years from that debacle, I continued to dream about a continuous footpath. It was 2001. I was general partner for a group holding 2,500 acres near Fort Pierce, and we had a planning and zoning issue that involved the state. I needed a good land use lawyer and someone suggested Wade Hopping in Tallahassee.

We had lunch after our meeting. Out of the blue I began telling Wade about our proposed 1,400 miles of hiking trails from one end of Florida to the other. By that time we had about 1,000 miles built, but we had picked the low-hanging fruit. We were adding 10 to 20 miles a year. Some years we lost more trail than we acquired.

I told Hopping that no one was encouraging the use of eminent domain for connecting sections of the trail. Even the Florida Trail Board of Directors was against the idea. But 30 years had passed. I wanted to try again. I wouldn't seek support from the Florida Trail board. I would do all this as one private citizen. Wade agreed to draft a bill pro bono.

The Florida Trail Association had a tenuous agreement with the Deseret Farms, owned by the Mormons. If we got written permission first, our members could traverse Florida Trail miles through Deseret Farms. This right of passage included a trail along the edge of the Kissimmee River flood plain, which was shaded by an almost continuous strand of huge live oaks—truly a gorgeous setting.

Two days after Hopping filed the bill, the FTA office received a letter from Deseret Farms, telling them to vacate the Mormons' stretch of trail. I received a phone call at once, telling me a group of board members wanted a meeting. They wanted me to pull the bill.

I tried to tell my supplicants that pressing the issue with the Mormons should make sense for them. The Mormons were land-planning these vast holdings for the development of a town someday in the future. Upland preservation would be required by the state. A hiking trail along the edge of the Kissimmee, which they couldn't develop anyway, would make sense as the trail became better known. Besides, any controversy would put the Florida Trail in the headlines. My friends weren't buying what I was selling.

I ended the meeting by proposing that they return to Gainesville, think about what I had said and call me in two weeks. Two weeks later their plea was the same. I told them I would pull the bill, then I would buy a sailboat, learn to sail and make my way to Europe. I bought the boat, learned how to sail and got as far as Bermuda. It was a terrific solo adventure.

But I wasn't about to abandon my dream for a continuous Florida Trail.

In 2008 I published a coffee table book on 50 years of wildlife photography. By the end of that decade I had started to look at a list of places I had been to go hiking and backpacking and to think about a companion volume that would fit in a sleeve with the first one. I surprised myself to find I had not only covered much of this country with my pack on, I had visited 22 other countries to do the same. *Trail Reflections: 50 Years of Hiking and Backpacking* was the result, published in 2012. It included a short essay in the appendix, titled "Is Your Favorite Trail Forever?" Here it is.

Is Your Favorite Trail Forever?

The hiking community has two urgent needs to protect their hiking trails, and I don't hear enough people talking about them. We need money to purchase privately owned gaps, and we need eminent domain for the gaps we can't close through negotiation.

So how and where do you start? The American Hiking Society has an annual Hike the Hill event in Washington, DC, where hikers rally for a week to visit with congresspeople and talk about appropriations. AHS staff briefs all newcomers, so they feel comfortable at the first office they visit. This is a great program, but it should be replicated in state houses across the country. Florida Trail members can attest to the success of this work, as can many others. To dramatize the need, the Pacific Crest Trail estimates $250 million is needed to acquire the trail's remaining 1,550 tracts. Yet Congress in 2012 only allocated $1 million, this for the second of two trails specifically mentioned in the 1968 act!

Money alone isn't enough. A trail must be continuous. Here, we come to the second need: eminent domain.

Every long-distance railroad, canal, power line, gas line, or road would never have been built through private property without the government's use of eminent domain when owners refuse to sell. The problem is that for most places, eminent domain for recreation does not exist. Hiking trails have yet to be considered a public need, like roads and rails.

The importance of trails is a cultural thing. We can learn a lot from the English. Hiking is part of a grand British tradition. As far back as 1826, Manchester formed the Association for the Preservation of Ancient Footpaths. The British passed the National Parks and Access to the Countryside Act 1949, which created additional rights for hikers. Later, the British passed the Countryside and Rights of Way Act 2000. You get the idea just from the titles.

Soon after I envisioned the creation of the Florida Trail, we mapped out the 1,500-mile route and built long sections of it to show what a public asset it would be. Thanks to numerous agreements with private property owners to cross their properties, we had a 1,000-mile trail within only a few years. No FTA members wanted to breathe the word "eminent domain" and disrupt the relationships that we had built. And things have remained in this limbo ever since. How do we bring up the idea of "taking" with people who have allowed us to cross their property? And how do we talk about "forever" without a taking?

A success story that should serve as a model for preserving trails is the Appalachian Trail. Construction began in the 1920s. By the '50s and '60s it was apparent that the trail would never be finished without eminent domain. After lengthy controversy, the National Trails System Act containing eminent domain for the A.T. was passed in 1968, but little happened. In 1978 Congress gave the National Park Service authority to go outside park boundaries and buy rights-of-way up and down the A.T. They then funded this effort with money from the Land and Water Conservation Fund. More than 111,000 acres in over 2,500 transactions have been acquired since then, through 2011. The U.S. Forest Service acquired an additional 56,700 acres. The two federal agencies have spent over $200 million on these acquisitions.

The key word in the title of this essay is "forever." We must work today—and uncounted tomorrows—for something we want for all time. When our government says they don't have any money, what they mean is they don't have any money for trails. We have to change that. Governments provide money for the common good and trails qualify. The total acreage needed is small, relative to other recreational uses or transportation corridors. Volunteers can usually be relied on to maintain the trails, once acquired.

To those who say now is not a good time, I say it's never a good time. By that I mean it's always a good time, because Congress is made up of people who often need to hear something two or a hundred times before they respond. Hikers can be practicing their lines today in "bad times" when "no one has any money," so when circumstances change, we will know our parts, have the play down pat and can tell our story again and again until we are heard, even if it takes a generation.

Hikers who support long-distance trails must face the fact that their trail will never be finished without the authority to take the last mile.

Eminent domain has been used along the A.T. not just in cases of an unwilling seller, but also to acquire properties with title defects and in estates without wills or a clear succession. In fact, few eminent domain cases are adversarial. Interestingly, only about 13% of the acquisition program required eminent domain, a total of about 415 parcels.

We must not be embarrassed by words like "condemnation," "taking," and "eminent domain," but must make these terms part our everyday vocabulary. We must market trails as the huge recreational bargain that they are. We must freely talk about the necessity of the "taking" process as essential and work it into our articles, books, programs and interviews. We must emphasize our trail as a "transportation corridor." We must sell the public on the necessity of seeing the corridor as deserving this authority. Without it, we labor in vain and our long-distance trails will never be completed.

Though we have a long way to go, we are on the right path. If hikers and their clubs lead the way, others will follow. The number of backpackers has jumped by 19% in the last five years. And 55 million Americans hike every year. There is also an economic aspect to our story. By 2011, hikers were spending more than $400 a year on their hobby. In Appendix 2 is a list of hiking clubs across America. Join a club. By becoming active in your local club, you will be pushing our trails closer and closer to protection "forever."

While Donald Trump was running for president, a reporter asked him what he thought about eminent domain. "I like it," he said. (There is more on this subject and the misuse of eminent domain in chapter two, but at first blush this was music to my ears. If Trump were elected, my dream might come true.) What action could I take to be prepared?

In 2013 I founded Hiking Trails for America with the stated purpose of closing the gaps in our National Scenic Trails. The A.T. was continuous and secure for posterity, but the other ten had gaps. I would have to try to find a board of directors that represented a broad base of influential hikers, who agreed with the mission. It was easier than I thought it would be.

Since I had founded the Florida Trail Association and therefore felt paternalistic toward it in a way I didn't feel toward the other National Scenic Trails, I also founded Friends of the Florida Trail a year after founding Hiking Trails for America, to concentrate extra effort on this one trail. The mission statements were the same.

Of course we had websites built to connect with social media. Sometimes we got things right on these websites. Sometimes we didn't. We are still working on this.

But my involvement with eminent domain goes back before that first Florida Trail hike in 1966. Toby Brigham and I were college classmates from 1952 to 1956. Toby then went to law school and returned to Miami to join his father's law firm, the largest eminent domain practice in the state. The state and federal governments were acquiring right-of-way for I-95 into downtown Miami in the early '60s and the Brighams represented most of the property owners whose land was taken. Toby asked this struggling land broker if I would be interested in photographing the properties they handled. These suits went on for years.

In the early 1990s I was representing the owners of 2,400 acres in St. Lucie County, Florida, when Florida Power & Light announced they were coming through the center of this huge tract with a 160-foot-wide power line easement. Eventually, this resulted in a negotiated settlement.

Yesterday in the mail I received a check in the low five figures (to the left of the decimal point), a partial payment for acreage taken to convert an entrance into Jacksonville International Airport from a two-lane road to a four-lane divided highway. So I have seen eminent domain close up for almost 60 years.

In 2016 Donald Trump was elected president. I waited anxiously, like many others, to see who was going to be selected as the Secretary of the Interior. I wanted a meeting to discuss closing the gaps in our National Scenic Trails. When Ryan Zinke was tapped, I waited a discreet several months and then wrote him. Months went by … but then I got a call from Zinke's office. Rick May was available to talk to me. Three of us on the Hiking Trails for America board met with May, a retired Navy Seal and a genuine person; but it was soon apparent that Trump and Zinke had a non-environmental agenda: open more federal lands to drilling and mining, shrink the size of some of our national monuments, ignore the data on climate science, among a long list that frightened environmentalists and nature lovers.

I have taken considerable space to make a point. For 60 years I have had long and diverse exposure to eminent domain and the issue of completing trails. In spite of the intentions of good trails people to complete our iconic trails through "negotiations and public and private partnerships," I can assure the reader it will never happen without significant money and the taking authority in the Bill of Rights. Remember, it's a corridor—like any other.

NOTES

1 "Trail Years: A History of the Appalachian Trail Conference." *Appalachian Trailway News*, Special 75th Anniversary Issue, pg. 56.

2 Private conversation with Don King, Chief, Land Acquisition Division, National Park Service.

3 This chart is not comprehensive and data has been culled from a number of state, federal and nonprofit sources as of January 2021

4 http://pnts.org/new/trinity-divide-deal-protects-17-miles-of-the-pacific-crest-trail/

https://www.pcta.org/2019/the-trinity-divide-land-acquisition-is-a-big-leap-toward-protecting-the-entire-pacific-crest-trail-66288/?fbclid=IwAR3q8tuEj0TqVKcszePgARVNEQ2POWAQTsB2Ttrj3N9NN-BDNS7EzL2iT5Q

5 https://www.pcta.org/wp-content/uploads/2018/06/2017-Land-Protection-Report-v3.pdf

6 Hiker registration information can be found on the Appalachian Trail Conservancy and Pacific Crest Trail websites.

7 16 USC § 1242(a)(2)

8 https://www.nps.gov/subjects/nationaltrailssystem/national-scenic-trails.htm

Differences noted in the charts, particularly mileages, may be traceable to different sources.

9 16 USC § 1242(b)

10 *The Mountains of California*, by John Muir. Published March 11, 1989, by Sierra Club Books (first published January 1, 1894).

11 https://www.backpacker.com/stories/wilderness-treatment-for-ptsd

12 *Grandma Gatewood's Walk: The Inspiring Story of the Woman Who Saved the Appalachian Trail*, by Ben Montgomery.

13 https://outdoorindustry.org/oia-participation/

14 Personal communication with Anne O'Neill, Outdoor Recreation Planner, National Park Service.

ACKNOWLEDGMENTS

The members of the board of Hiking Trails for America have been a huge help with this project. Bill Kemsley, Larry Luxenberg and Paul Pritchard, the executive committee, have helped with overviews, details in every chapter, even the title. Dennis Lewon weighed in at the end with comments that might go into another book. He also helped with suggestions for the title, as did Ron Strickland. Their collective thoughts were more important than they realize.

Amalie Parrott supplied data and roamed the manuscript looking for facts that needed checking. Lonna Allen was reviewing this product daily, typing new pages when they were ready, always with a can-do attitude, never getting flustered or out of sorts. Thank goodness I had Beth Mansbridge copyediting the manuscript. I hadn't spoken to Caroline Blochlinger in years. She formatted and designed two other books for me but, that was years ago. Fortunately, she was available. A real dream team.

Board of Hiking Trails for America:
William Kemsley
Larry Luxenberg
Paul Pritchard
Ron Strickland
Dennis Lewon
Catherine Stratton
Peter Metcalf

Jim Kern

About the Author

Jim Kern has been an avid hiker and backpacker since 1961. In 1966 he founded the Florida Trail and the Florida Trail Association. In 1976 he co-founded the American Hiking Society with Bill Kemsley, founding editor and publisher of *Backpacker* magazine, and Paul Pritchard, then president of the Appalachian Trail Conference. In 1989 Kern founded Big City Mountaineers, a high-adventure backpacking program for disadvantaged inner-city teens.

In 2012 the author published *Trail Reflections: 50 Years of Hiking and Backpacking*. This coffee table book recounts, in text and in over 400 color photographs, hiking adventures on Mount Kinabalu in Borneo, a hike from the Karakoram Highway to Shimshal in northern Pakistan, on a circular route of Torres del Paine in Tierra del Fuego and on the Milford Track, South Island, New Zealand, among others.

In 2013 Kern formed Hiking Trails for America (www.hikingtrailsinamerica.org) to support permanent protection and continuity for all National Scenic Trails. In 2014 he formed Friends of the Florida Trail (www.friendsoffloridatrail.org) to promote the acquisition of a continuous right-of-way for the Florida Trail.

Jim Kern grew up in Leonia, New Jersey. He attended Andover and Yale and moved to Florida in 1958. He has been a real estate broker since 1960, specializing in brokering, buying and selling vacant Florida land. He lives in St. Augustine, Florida, and Highlands, North Carolina